Living
with
Conviction

Living with Conviction

German Army Captain Turns to Cultivating Peace

by

Siegfried Bartel

CMBC Publications
Winnipeg, Manitoba
1994

CMBC Publications
600 Shaftesbury Blvd
Winnipeg, Manitoba
R3P 0M4

Cover: Gerald Loewen

Canadian Cataloguing in Publication Data

Bartel, Siegfried, 1915--

Living with conviction

Includes bibliographical references.
ISBN: 0-920718-51-5

1. Bartel, Siegfried, 1915--   2. Mennonites -- British Columbia -- Biography. 3. German Canadians -- British Columbia -- Biography. 4. Mennonite Central Committee. I. Title

BX8143.B37A3   1994   289.7'092   C94--920223--1

Printed in Canada
by
Friesen Printers
Altona, Manitoba
R0G 0B0

Contents

Acknowledgements   viii
Foreword   ix
Looking Back   xii

I. Growing Up in West Prussia

1. Born in a World at War   2
2. My Parents   2
3. Childhood: Paradise and Joy   5
4. Childhood: Darkness and Tears   7
5. My Second Family   8
6. My Older Brothers and Sisters   10
7. My Younger Siblings   12
8. The Farm at Reichfelde   14
9. Help with the Farming   16
10. The Farmer as Manager   18
11. Caught in the System   19
12. Participation in Church Life   20
13. Testing My Faith   21
14. Establishing Credentials   23
15. Foretaste of the Future   25

II. War Is Hell

16. Joining the Army   28
17. Engagement midst Clouds of War   30
18. The War Begins   34
19. War Academy—Wedding at Christmas   36
20. New Life between Battles   39
21. The Beginning of the End   41
22. My Darkest Hour   46
23. Our Saddest Day   49
24. The Bitter End   53

III. Trying to Put Things Back Together Again

25. New Beginnings   58
26. Reunited with My Family   60
27. Post-War Struggles   63
28. Farming in Dörphof   67
29. First Experiences in Public Life   69
30. Decision to Leave   70
31. Where to Now?   73
32. Destination Canada   76
33. Voyage across the Ocean   81

IV. Finding a Way of Life in Canada: Family, Farm and Faith

34. From East to West   86
35. Farming on Our Own   88
36. The Bartel-Andres Partnership   93
37. The Bartel Brothers Operation   103
38. Our Six Sons   105
39. Church Life in Agassiz   111
40. Back to Family Farming   116

V. Entering the Public Arena

41. An Immigrant on the School Board   122
42. Advocate for the Doukhobors   127
43. Beginning Inter-Mennonite Involvements   135
44. First Foray into MCC Work   135

VI. Working in the Second Level of MCC

45. For Whom Do I Speak?   144
46. The Vote on Capital Punishment   144
47. Inter-Office Relations   146
48. An MCC Presence in Ottawa   148
49. Submission to the Deschenes Commission   149
50. How Does MCC Share the Gospel?   152
51. Responsibility to Canada's Native People   153
52. End of Service   154

VII. Moving beyond Canadian Boundaries with MCC

53. Withholding My Vote — 158
54. MCC and Europe — 159
55. Participation in Peace Demonstrations — 163
56. Assistance to Bruno Schottstädt — 165
57. Work with Umsiedler — 166
58. Back to My Roots — 167
59. Policy on Relief — 169
60. Learning about MCC in South America — 170
61. Seeing MCC at Work in Asia — 173
62. Personnel in Contested Areas — 175
63. Policy on Abstinence — 178
64. Farewell to MCC — 179

VIII. Sharing My Story

65. The End of Farming — 184
66. Diary of Preaching-Teaching Assignments — 187
    November 1988: Saskatchewan — 188
    March 1989: Manitoba — 188
    April 1989: U.S. East Coast — 189
    September 1989: Ontario — 191
    October 1989: Alberta — 192
    March 1990: U.S. West Coast — 192
    October 1990: U.S. Great Lakes — 193
    January 1991: Ohio — 193
    July 1990: Brethren in Christ Conference — 194
    October 1991: Elkhart-Goshen — 195
    November 1991: Bethel Mennonite Church — 197
67. Reflections of an Unordained Person — 197
68. The Road to Forgiveness — 201

Looking Ahead — 206

Words of Thanksgiving — 208
Book References — 212

Acknowledgements

I want to acknowledge and say "Thank you" to all those who encouraged me to write my life story. To John H. Redekop, who did that in a very direct way; to many friends—I name one as a representative of all of them—my farmer friend Roger Kennel who served with me as a member of the MCC (binational) board.

Thank you to Regina, our daughter-in-law, who enthusiastically keyed the manuscript into the computer and was able to decipher my handwriting and improve on writing style. Thank you also to Gerd for helping her. Thank you as well to the members of MCC Canada staff who gave their time in entering sections of the first revised manuscript into the computer.

I thank Margaret Franz in a special way for editing, rearranging and shortening my manuscript in preparation for submitting it to the publisher.

Special thanks to my friend Larry Kehler for being a great encouragement in my pilgrimage and in my work with the Conference of Mennonites in Canada and in MCC, but mainly for being my mentor in editing the manuscript and giving guidance for publishing this book.

To all, my heartfelt thanks!

Siegfried Bartel
Agassiz, British Columbia
August 1994

Foreword

Siegfried Bartel is a rare human being. In these pages you will discover a master farmer, whether in pre-World War II West Prussia, in post-war Schleswig-Holstein or, since 1951, in British Columbia, Canada. In these pages you meet a devout Christian nurtured in a Prussian Mennonite congregation, Thiensdorf-Rosengart, and expressed in conscious discipleship, whether on the farm, in the military, or as congregational and denominational leader. In these pages you will admire a conscientious husband, father and grandfather. I am delighted that Siegfried was persuaded to share his life story so honestly and unassumingly.

To know Siegfried is to know a person with strong convictions. Some are expressed in these pages. To know Siegfried is to know a person of deep empathy to human suffering, nurtured in a life that has seen and experienced pain close at hand. To know Siegfried is to know a person who has grown at every stage of life to deeper and broader expressions of Christian faith.

One thing that makes this story so interesting is Siegfried's Prussianness. As with everyone, the first decades of Siegfried's life set a style. Prussians love the land. Siegfried proudly carries the label of farmer. He loves horses and, like his father, bred fine Holstein cattle. Prussia has a class-oriented society. Siegfried agonized over well-established personal and familial roles and distinctions. He was humble enough to learn bottom-up farming in British Columbia. Prussians have a strong sense of family. The ancestry of the Bartels, Andres and Sieberts goes back to Dutch Mennonite colonists who, in the 16th century, brought religious devotion and agricultural development skills to Poland's Vistula Delta. Prussians have a long military tradition. Siegfried and his Mennonite friends got caught up in this "system." Much of the drama of this memoir is generated by the tension between a peaceful tradition and this Prussianness.

Prussians are also known for their piety. For most, this was Lutheran. But for 400 years there was a small, vigorous Mennonite community which was the motherland for most Mennonites in

Russia and Ukraine, most Mennonites in Uruguay and substantial congregations in the United States and Canada. Many Prussian Mennonites were deeply impacted by Pietist lay spirituality in the 18th and 19th centuries. Siegfried's parents passed on this tradition to their children. Their piety made interaction with Lutheran neighbours easy but it also made fuzzy the boundaries with German nationalism. Yet it is important to note that Erna Bartel's father, Emil Siebert, "uncompromising in his interpretation of scripture and history," was one of the few Mennonite lay ministers who taught biblical non-resistance right down to World War II.

Siegfried Bartel's "rocky journey from unawareness to conviction" took place amidst some of the pivotal movements of the 20th century. True to his strong sense of civic responsibility, he joined the German Army in 1937. He quickly climbed the leadership ladder. Twice wounded, he was twice given the Iron Cross for valour and leadership. In his first combat in September 1939, he wondered about shelling the Polish town where his father had attended school and the possibility of meeting a cousin serving in the Polish Army. On a haunting December 25, 1941, on the Russian front he heard "the enemy" soldiers singing Christmas carols. From then on his ambivalence about war as a solution for human problems began to increase. In the midst of combat, death and defeat, this sensitive individual decided he was on the wrong track. In later years, as one who experienced forgiveness for being involved in the German Army, Siegfried would make eloquent appeals for peace. Now we know he is apprehensive that North American Mennonites are being engulfed by the system he struggled to escape.

Every life must be understood in context. If Prussia, the Reichfelde estate, military service, war, refugee wanderings dominated the formative years, the mature years for Siegfried and Erna's life were dominated by getting established in Canada, raising six sons, becoming a British Columbia dairy farmer, being an active participant in community life including the school board and parole board, taking on leadership in the Eden Mennonite congregation and the various boards of the Mennonite Central Committee.

These memoirs not only tell a story but provide teasing insights into contemporary North American Mennonite church life. As a wise layman, for example, he observed four kinds of spiritual arrogance: the arrogance of the office of ordination, the arrogance of organizational power, the arrogance of intellect and the arrogance of being educated. Rarely has anyone within the Mennonite tradition been so clear in assessing the weakness of ordained leadership. Siegfried briefly notes the problem of board leadership in an established organization like Mennonite Central Committee. Members of other boards will learn here the time it takes to be a good committee member and how to dissent with courage and grace when there are genuine reasons for disagreement.

One of the special joys of my life has been to know Siegfried Bartel. I hope many more people will get to know this remarkable person by reading this wonderful testimony of faith, not as theological argument, but rather as a pilgrimage of worship and holy living. Siegfried and Erna Bartel raised their sons "to be different than the majority of young people." This book is a fascinating story of a life-long search to be different for the glory of God.

John A. Lapp
Executive Secretary
Mennonite Central Committee
Akron, Pennsylvania
August 1, 1994

Looking Back

I sit here in my comfortable home on the edge of the mountains overlooking the Fraser Valley in British Columbia. Surrounded by the rocky grandeur, my life passes before my eyes.

My journey often took me over rough roads and unclear paths. I recall my childhood days in Reichfelde, West Prussia, and life on the farm there. Back then my decision to join the German Army seemed like a natural step. By now my experiences after the Second World War as farm manager in Dörphof, Germany, are in the distant past. How could I know then that soon we would be crossing the ocean to Canada, that the farm experience in Germany was preparing me to be a farmer here in Agassiz, British Columbia?

I remember those first months as a member, then my years as chairman, on the Agassiz-Harrison School Board. Little did I know how many meetings I would attend over the years. And, even though I had struggles with the organized church, most of those meetings would be with major church-related organizations. Who could have told me that I would make some of my best friends by challenging their thinking? That I would be asked to travel across this country and beyond to speak about God's working in my life?

Through all those experiences I was always assured of the support of Ernusch, my wife for over 50 years, and of our six sons, daughters-in-law, grandchildren and extended family.

Some memories are beginning to fade; others remain clear. But as I recall my life and ponder its meaning, there is one memory which will never leave me—one incident during the war which has shaped who I am, how I think and what I do. One experience changed my life completely. And that change is the story of this book.

I invite you to join me on my rocky journey from unawareness to conviction, from guilt to assurance of forgiveness, from struggle to victory.

Let me begin at the beginning . . .

I

Growing Up in West Prussia

My mother died when I was seven years old. I re-member the years of mourning as a time of tears and prayers. The new era, when my stepmother came to us, I remember as a time of adjustment and prayer. But with father as a constant example of courage and dedication, Reichfelde, our farm es-tate, became like a heaven on earth for us children.

1. Born in a World at War

On December 15, 1914, my mother wrote in her diary: "I am feeling healthy and content during this time of waiting for the birth of my child. My heart is filled with joy, O Lord. Bless this child."

I was born three weeks later, January 6, 1915, on my parents' farm in Reichfelde, West Prussia. World War I had just begun to rage across Europe. It was a time of great fear for the people in East and West Prussia. According to my mother's diary, they had made preparations to flee in case there would be direct military action in their area. The Battle of Tannenberg, in which the German forces under the command of Hindenburg were victorious over the Russian army, brought this fear to an end.

I was the fifth child of Heinrich and Agathe (nee Andres) Bartel. My older siblings, Walter, Hanna, Magdalena and Gretel, were born in Klettendorf, approximately five kilometres from the Reichfelde estate (*Hof*). My parents had bought the new farm so they would have more land, and also to provide room for expansion. Mother did not appreciate the move. Notes written by my father indicate that she "shed many tears about the change."

My brother Hans was the first child born in Reichfelde (1912). After my arrival, three more children were born into our family between 1917 and 1921: Ruth, Heinz-Otto and Reinhard. One of my mother's anxieties about leaving Klettendorf was, that when they bought the estate, there was only a mud road leading to the farm house. She was concerned that the midwife would have transportation problems at the time of my arrival.

2. My Parents

My mother *(Mutti)*, Agathe Andres, was born in 1881 in Einlage (Robach). Her parents had a farm combined with a wind-driven mill and a grocery store. She had one sister and three brothers. The boys went to private Christian residential schools, but mother received her main education at a private school in Neuteich. That is where she learned English, a language in which she became proficient in her teens. In fact, Mutti sometimes wrote her diary and also poems in that language.

Her parents' marriage relationship was not ideal, but mother's obedience to them never wavered. She was very close to her brother Johannes who died at the age of 19. His death had a profound influence on mother's spiritual life. She wrote a song for his funeral which later was sung at her own burial.

In her early teens Mutti had accepted the Lord as her personal Saviour. The Pietist movement had a strong influence on her spiritual pilgrimage, an influence which motivated her to evangelize within the family circle and beyond. At age 18 she started a mission sewing circle of about 15 young women.

I am sure I learned my first prayer from my mother's lips: "Ich bin klein, mein Herz mach rein; Soll niemand drin wohnen, als Jesus allein" (I am small, cleanse my heart. Let no one take possession of it except Jesus alone). Her close friend, Hanna Wiehler, who became her sister-in-law and later our stepmother, told us that she had been led to the Lord by my mother.

My father *(Vati)*, Heinrich Bartel, the third of eight children, was born in Lubin, West Prussia. He must have been quite self-assured because as a young man he became known as "the proud Heinrich."

Vati met my mother for the first time when the young members of the Andres family visited the Mennonite young people in the Graudenz area. He was about 16 at the time. In his memoirs he wrote that he told his sisters after that visit: "You know, Agathe Andres could be the girl I would like to marry." During his later education Vati attended an agricultural school in Zoppot near Gdansk. While there, he had contact with Mennonite youth in the Danzig area and met my mother again.

He wrote in his memoirs: "The two of us were the only young people who did not dance, so we had a lot of time to walk in the garden and talk. My love for her grew, but we did not talk about that."

About another meeting Vati's diary entry stated: "On that occasion I asked her about the book of poems she had written. I thought they would help me understand her spiritual thoughts better." The correspondence that developed after that shows the deep spirituality which influenced both of their lives.

On January 24, 1904, the year of their marriage, Mutti wrote in her diary (in English): "This morning we both prayed together. Oh, I am so happy that we have the same faith and trust in our Saviour.

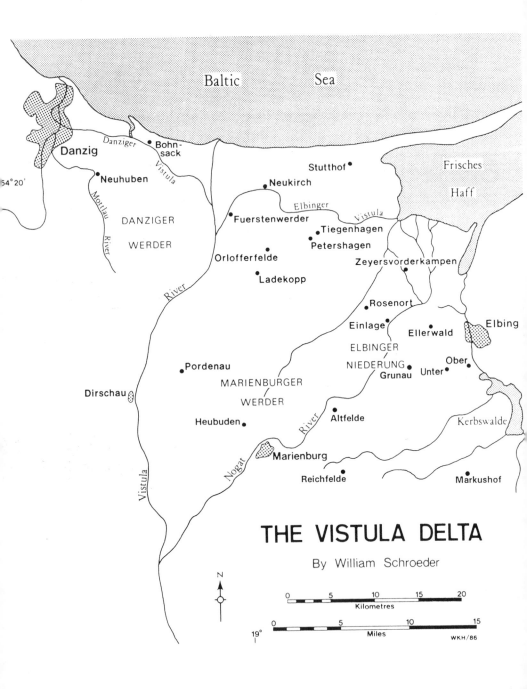

THE VISTULA DELTA

By William Schroeder

Adapted from William Schroeder's map in Mennonite Historical Atlas. Maps by William Schroeder, text by Helmut T. Huebert. Winnipeg, Canada, 1990.

*My parents, Agathe
(Andres) & Heinrich
Bartel, April 1912*

Every time we've been together I feel happier. Praise the Lord, O my soul!"

3. Childhood: Paradise and Joy

In my early years, Reichfelde was a child's paradise. The village was three kilometres south of Altfelde, the train station, and our estate was located a further three kilometres west of the village. The farm was situated along the dike of the Thiene River, a brook in which we children loved to play during the summer months. It became a deep and muddy stream during spring runoff. Altfelde was one of the two train stations between Elbing and Marienburg, the two cities that played an important role in our lives. That railroad was the main track connecting Königsberg to Berlin.

On the road between the village Reichfelde and our estate were two neighbouring farms. Uncle Gustav Andres (Mutti's cousin), Aunt Luischen and their family lived on one farm, Frau Janzen and her daughter Anneli on the other. Across the Thiene River were Polish neighbours who had much smaller farms. Although they lived only a few hundred yards away, we had little contact with them.

Reichfelde, the estate where I was born in 1915 near the village of Altfelde in West Prussia.

The road from Reichfelde to our farm continued west to Schroop, the home of mother's brother, Uncle Jacob Andres and Aunt Anna. Aunt Anna was our *Lieblingstante* (beloved aunt). I received my first schooling at a private school in their house.

The school year always began right after Easter. I was only five when I began my formal education, driving the five kilometres to Schroop every day by horse and buggy with my brother Hans. My older sisters went to the home of Uncle Gustav and Aunt Luischen Andres for their education where Miss Schilling was the teacher.

In spite of my tender age, I enjoyed a good prank. I knew that my teacher, Miss Eisenblätter, was terrified of dogs. Her desk in the classroom was covered with a large tablecloth which hung down to the floor. One morning I hid under the desk and, when she entered the room, I barked like a dog, causing her to run from the room in fright. We had a hard time convincing her that there was in fact no dog in the room.

I don't remember what she did to me in response to that prank, but I do recall another occasion. When I had not behaved according to her standards, she sent me outside. I accepted the fact that I was not wanted, went to the barn, hitched up the pony and drove home, much to the surprise of my parents. One of the farm workers, the coachman, then had to drive the buggy back to Schroop to pick up my brother Hans.

For my second and third school years I went to the private school in our own home. The teacher, Mr. Fischer, was the best instructor of my private school life. He was a hunter. When weather and time permitted, I was allowed to accompany him on his hunting trips.

Our estate had a large farmhouse with 16 rooms, including 12 bedrooms. We felt very comfortable there. The bedrooms for the younger children were on both sides of the parents' bedroom, the younger girls on one side and the boys on the other. The upstairs was divided into two sections. David Rempel, our farm manager, and his family lived in two rooms in the southern part. My older sisters and some of the female servants had their bedrooms on the north end.

The large table in the dining room could seat approximately two dozen people but it was not always full. In my early childhood I remember that the maids ate in the kitchen. Later that arrangement was changed. The unmarried young men who worked with the horses had their sleeping quarters in the barn. They ate in a room in the basement which had a separate entrance. We children discovered early on that there was a special bond between the young unmarried farm hands and the maids working in the house.

We usually had two maids, one helping in the kitchen, the other taking care of the house cleaning. A third woman helped look after the smaller children. The class system was taken for granted at that time and influenced our lives in a wide range of relationships.

One member of the staff, Miss Platt—Platy we called her—belonged to a class which was different than any other on the estate. She had come from the city. Her first job at Reichfelde was as a private nurse, taking care of Mutti's aging mother. After grandmother's death, Platy remained as Mutti's assistant in the large household. In a letter which Mutti wrote in 1919 to the Andres relatives living in Kansas, U.S.A., she mentioned that she had to cook meals for 30 people every day—14 residents in the house and 16 workers. Platy was a big help to Mutti but to us children she became like an older sister whom we loved very much.

4. Childhood: Darkness and Tears

Reichfelde was like a heaven on earth for us, but that paradise was shattered when I was only seven years old. On April 7, 1922, a tragic accident darkened our lives. A collision at a train crossing took the life of Mutti and my oldest brother, Walter. Walter was killed instantly; Mother died from her injuries five weeks later in the Elbing Hospital. Vati and brother Hans survived the mishap without serious injury.

The man in charge of closing the gates at the train crossing had been drunk that dark and stormy night, and had fallen asleep. Walter, who was driving the horse and buggy, did not notice the approaching train, resulting in the traumatic collision.

Early the next morning a messenger came on horseback from Grunau to bring us the sad news. Platy, our nanny and friend, took us children to our parents' bed and explained what had happened. The picture of the messenger's horse tied to the picket fence on our yard is still vividly etched into my memory. I remember visiting Mother only once at the hospital in Elbing.

At the funeral the coffin stood in the middle of our *grosse Stube,* a room in the house which was used only for larger gatherings such as birthdays, sewing bees (*Nähstunden*), evangelistic meetings and Christmas celebrations. In the procession to the cemetery in Altfelde, I sat beside the coachman (*Kutscher*) on the first wagon behind the cart carrying the coffin. From my vantage point I could see that when we arrived in the village of Reichfelde, the last buggy was just leaving the driveway of our farm three kilometres away.

Vati shed many tears during the next few years, but not even then did he forget his sense of justice. The court case against the man who had been in charge of the gate at the train crossing became a sensational story. Vati pleaded with the judge to spare the accused man from punishment. First, he said, Mutti could not be brought back to life through a jail term; secondly, the guilt which the man would have to carry for the rest of his life was punishment enough.

5. My Second Family

Grandmother (*Oma*) Bartel had been living with Vati's brother Otto and family in Grunau. After Mutti's death she came to Reichfelde to help Vati with looking after the house and raising the family. She was a very tall woman and I remember her as a person gaining respect merely through her appearance. When Oma died in 1925, only three years after Mutti's death, raising the family was left to Vati and the older sisters. This may be why I do not remember these sisters as ever being young. Grieving the death of loved ones and taking on family responsibilities overshadowed their youth.

As an eight-year-old shortly after Mutti died in 1922.

From my early childhood I do not remember anyone from our circle of relatives more fondly than Uncle Gustav Andres, one of my mother's two brothers. We called him Uncle Gos. He was married to Tante Hanna, who had been Mutti's close friend even before she married my father. It was always a special time when Uncle Gos and Tante Hanna, with their daughter Trautchen, came to visit us. During those years the automobile was being introduced to our communities. Uncle Gos owned a special type of vehicle, a three-wheeler. It had comfortable seats and a steering apparatus with a large handle attached to the front wheel. The throttle control was on the steering column. Onkel Gos always gave us special rides, but he also paid attention to us personally. When he came home from his time of serving in one of the army's Red Cross units, he had developed a kidney disease and died only a year after the train accident which had taken the life of my mother and brother Walter.

Vati had become a widower before he reached his fortieth birthday. He had eight children with Reinhard, the youngest, only 18 months old at the time. Vati and Mutti had enjoyed a very close relationship. Therefore, anyone who might take Mutti's place would have to live with the past and could not expect to receive Vati's full attention and love, at least for a while. A second concern for any would-be spouse must have been his large family.

As one of the younger children in the family, I was not aware of Vati's concerns related to the future of his life and family. Platy and my older sisters were looking after us very well. What a surprise and how happy we all were when we heard that Tante Hanna from Elbing would be coming to marry Vati and to be our mother. Tante Hanna must have found it very difficult to make the decision to come to Reichfelde and take our mother's place. She had been happy in her marriage to the kind and caring Uncle Gos. It would be an enormous adjustment to live with Vati, who was a more reserved family patriarch.

The wedding took place in December 1925. A severe snowstorm forced the cancellation of the church ceremony.

Vati's remarriage resulted in significant changes. Not only did we have a mother again—we called her *Muttchen*—but Trautchen, our cousin, became our sister. An additional bonus for us was that Tante Hanna brought along *The Brennabor*, the most modern automobile of that day.

During our three years without a mother, Platy had taken charge of the large household and had stepped into the mother role for us younger children. We had become very attached to her. Now I understand why she had to leave Reichfelde to make room for Muttchen to establish authority in the large household and to open up avenues for building a close relationship to us children. At the time we did not understand why Platy had to go. Deep within, some of the children felt resentment toward Muttchen for having taken our beloved nanny from us. When Platy left for the train station, the smaller children stood around the buggy in front of the house, crying.

6. My Older Brothers and Sisters

Walter, the firstborn in our family, received his education at a high school in Elbing. I remember how Vati looked forward to the time when Walter would join the farm after achieving the *Ein-jährige* (a grade ten diploma). We all admired him for his educational achievement. He had a lively temperament, and we all looked forward to him coming home for weekends. When he died instantly in the train accident on April 7, 1922, I remember how Vati took me on his lap and said, "Now you are my little Walter." Apparently I looked a bit like Walter and was the only other boy in the family with a rough complexion like his (Genesis 27:11).

My three older sisters, Hanna, Magdalena and Gretel, as different as they were, represented to us younger ones the mature type of sisters who did not know what it meant to be young—at least that's how it seemed to me.

Hanna, who was 14 when Mutti and Walter died, then became the oldest child in our family. This fact influenced her life in many ways. Even though Oma Bartel moved from Grunau to Reichfelde to become head of the household and Platy was responsible for the everyday activities in the large farm house, Hanna became the natural closest companion to Vatchen during his three-and-a-half years as a widower. That changed somewhat when our family rented an apartment in Marienburg while five of us went to high school there. Hanna took over the parenting role during the week and devoted the best years of her life to the welfare of the family. No wonder her whole life involved serving others.

Magdalena (Marlenchen) had her own way of presenting herself. Convinced that she was the prettiest of the three older sisters, she carried herself with the air of a queen. Magdalena's wedding to Paul Schneiderreit in Reichfelde was a huge affair. It was said that during the time of their engagement, when she was undressing at bedtime, she would turn his picture toward the wall. We younger ones occasionally inspected Paul's picture to see if there were any signs of Magdalena's lips on the glass. Eventually, they settled on a farm in East Prussia until she and the farm workers fled to Reichfelde because of the war. She was part of the trek to Hoheneggelsen. In 1946 Magdalena and Paul settled in Dortmund, West Germany.

Gretel always remained in the background when she was with her two sisters. As a teenager she developed tuberculosis and went to the healing environment of Davos in Switzerland. There she worked for a pastor's family, von Rechenberg. During the war she, together with Trautchen and Hanna, managed the large farm household in Reichfelde. Gretel had become engaged to Abraham Harder who was widowed in Paraguay shortly before the war. It took seven years before she could join the first transport of Mennonite refugees from Russia going to Paraguay to marry Abraham, a well-known and highly respected Bible teacher and elder. Her health could not tolerate the climate in Paraguay so they emigrated to Canada in 1951, the same year we arrived.

Hans, who is three years older than I, related more to the three older sisters than to us younger ones. Early every morning for four years the two of us and the neighbour's daughter, drove seven kilometres by horse and buggy to the station in Altfelde. There we boarded the train to Marienburg where we went to school. Hans became farm manager at Reichfelde. Those were the years when Annchen Kröker from Wernigerode, a friend of my sisters, came to our estate for the summer holidays. To develop closer contact, Annchen and I engaged in an intensive exchange of letters which was actually meant for Hans. Later he continued this contact, tentatively at first, but then with growing enthusiasm.

7. My Younger Siblings

Ruth was always the well behaved one among the children, especially in the eyes of the adults. The two of us enjoyed a comfortable companionship, especially in Marienburg where we were the two older ones in the family group. In her early teens she left Reichfelde to go into nurses' training and later to the conservatory in Berlin to study organ. After her marriage to Ernst Schroeder, she accepted a job as organist in Hoheneggelsen. That was a contributing factor to our family's decision later to move all the way to that town in Germany.

Gertraut, Trautchen we called her, came to Reichfelde with our second mother. A cousin thus became a sister. It must have been difficult for her to share her mother's time and love with so many family members. Our watchful eyes were eager to detect any special treatment from Muttchen. As teenagers, Trautchen and I developed an additional closeness when my future life's partner, Erna Siebert, became her friend. My pen pal, Waldemar Hörr, became interested in Gertraut, and they were married in the fall of 1939. Waldemar went missing in action in Russia during the war.

Heinz-Otto (Heinrich-Otto) bore the name of Vati as well as his brother Otto. He was very sickly as a child and developed an especially close relationship to Platy. Perhaps that was why he had a more difficult time relating to Muttchen than the rest of us. After the war ended, he spent much time and effort trying to find Platy, but without success. In 1947-48 he studied agriculture in Kiel. Heinz-Otto resembled our father in his appearance, but there were also some fundamental differences between them. Even though an inner tender-

Muttchen (our stepmother) with part of her new family in 1925 (from left): Siegfried, Ruth, Reinhard (front), Hans (back), Gertraut (Muttchen's daughter), Heinz-Otto. The older three sisters are missing from photo.

ness was part of his being, at times a hint of aggressiveness was also apparent in him.

Reinhard was only 18 months when Mutti died. I can still see him as a pre-schooler with his long blonde curls, sitting on the steps of the granary with his dolls in his arms, daydreaming. Of all the children from Vatchen's first marriage he was the one who had the closest relationship with Muttchen. He also became very close to Hanna during the time they lived together in Marienburg.

Eva-Marie was the firstborn of the marriage of Vati and Muttchen. She died when she was only two weeks old. Hers was the first death I witnessed.

Walter Gustav was born when I was 14. As a child he was not very strong, yet he was considered healthy enough to be drafted into the army just before the war ended. The British released him, a young prisoner of war, early. In Canada we became long-time farming partners.

Rudolf Wiebler, whose father Gustav was Muttchen's brother, came to live with us in Reichfelde after his parents were divorced. Age-wise he was between Reinhard and Walter. He was a pleasant boy, but somewhat shy and could not fully feel at home anywhere. He joined the army early and went missing in action in Stalingrad.

8. The Farm at Reichfelde

Since Mennonites had experience in farming the lowlands, they settled in the Vistula and Nogat delta regions of Prussia. Earlier they had lived mainly on smaller farms. My parents' generation was the first to own larger ones. Our estate at Reichfelde was one such major farming operation. Besides the 16-room farmhouse was the large brick barn with a clay tile roof. The first section of the barn housed the chickens and geese; then came the unloading area for potatoes for the pigs. The pig barn was on the south side with space for the buggies on the north side. We had seven different buggies, several of them already having rubber tires. Adjacent to this area was the horse stable, then the cow barn. The granary, which was located between the buggy shed and the entrance to the pig pens, contained the entrance to the second and third stories of the barn. The total length of the barn was approximately 70 metres.

Next to the barn were two large wooden sheds *(Scheunen),* each about 70 metres long and 20 metres wide. Both sheds had large doors so that during harvest time a fully loaded wagon with sheaves could enter. We owned the most advanced harvesting equipment at that time which was a horse-drawn binder that cut the standing grain and bound it into sheaves. The bundles were then put up into little stacks in the field and left to dry for several days.

During harvest our old-fashioned farm wagons, which were normally used to transport beets, potatoes and even manure, were converted into hayracks (*Leiterwagen*). These wagons, built of heavy lumber, had steel axles and wheels with modern wooden spokes. For harvest, extensions (*Leitern*) were added between the front and rear axles. Then they were driven along the rows of stacks where two men with forks threw the sheaves up into the wagon. Usually two women were on the wagon stacking the sheaves so the load would remain in place during the drive to the sheds.

We children usually had the job called *weiterrücken*, which involved driving the horses from one stack of sheaves to the next. Sometimes when we didn't stop in time or got too close or not close enough to the sheaves, the men responsible for doing the loading would throw pieces of dirt at us as we sat on the saddle horse. When a boy reached the age of eight, he was promoted from the tiresome job of *weiterrücken* to doing the raking. The horse-drawn rake followed the wagon to clean the field after the sheaves had been loaded and to bring the loose grain to the wagon for loading.

During harvest time some grain was taken from the field directly to the threshing machine, which was either standing in the large shed or outside. To speed up harvesting, more than half of the sheaves were put into storage in the sheds. The stored sheaves were threshed during the winter when there was less time pressure. These large sheds on the farm were also the main places for us boys to amuse ourselves. We would play hide 'n seek or jump from the high beams into the loose straw.

On the north end of the older *Scheune* were a woodshed and the *Rollkammer* where the women workers looked after the laundry. When they had washed bed sheets and towels, they took the dry linen to the *Rollkammer,* which contained the so-called *Rolle* (roller or mangle). By turning a large handle, a heavy, rock-filled box was rolled across the top of the table for approximately two metres on wooden rollers ten-centimetres in diameter. It was the women's job to place the wooden rolls, with linen rolled around them, under the box. This process was a simple and effective method of pressing the linen.

Right beside the *Rollkammer* was the tool shed for field work. Kollikowski, who was in charge of the tools, had his workshop around the corner from that building. He always kept an eye on the tools, counted them in the evening after work, replaced broken handles and sharpened hoes. The regular farm workers had their own tools and kept them, especially the scythes, in good repair.

On the north side of our house was a large, park-like garden. It had flower beds, fruit trees, shrubs and large lawns. The walkways were kept clean and the edges of the lawns were neatly trimmed. Along the dike of the Thiene River on the west end of the garden was the Thiene wall, parallel hedges with one row of fir trees and another of cedars, about 120 metres long. Close to the west side of the house were two large chestnut trees with a heavy, four-metre high beam fastened between them. Attached to it was a swing which provided a lot of entertainment for children and young people.

The children of the family were responsible to help in the garden and do other regular chores. In summer all the walkways, some parts of the front yard and the five-metre wide cobblestone path beside the barn had to be cleaned with a broom for the weekend and also when visitors were expected. There was an unspoken competition, at least among some relatives, for cleanliness and neatness on the farm. We boys spent many hours washing the tails of the milk cows, particularly for special occasions. The straw on the farmyard which had been missed by the hand-rakes had to be picked up by the children.

The welfare of our animals was always a major concern. Everyone who was in charge of a certain section of the farming operation looked after the animals under his supervision, but in the evening before bedtime someone from the family or the farm manager (*Inspektor*) would walk through all the barns and check on the animals. This activity was called *ableuchten*. I assume this practice originated at a time when lanterns were used for light. Of course we already had electricity.

9. Help with the Farming

Characteristic of West Prussian farming, farm life at Reichfelde was a mixture with something of everything. We grew rye, sugar beets, potatoes, barley, oats and huge quantities of beets, which were the basic feed for cattle in wintertime.

Manual labour was much more important then. Therefore the number of labourers varied according to the season. Seven men made up the permanent farm staff, each being responsible for a different area of work on the estate. These workers and their families lived in small houses on the estate. Each also had a small barn in which they raised a few pigs for their own use, or sometimes to sell. They also had chickens, geese and goats for extra milk. In addition to their wages, the workers received a supply of milk daily, and flour and grain monthly. They made their own hay along the ditches and dikes of the Thiene River and received coal and wood for cooking and heating. There was a small field of alfalfa where they could all cut grass for their own animals during the summer.

Some of these workers stayed at Reichfelde for many years and became almost like part of the family. I remember each of them. It was custom on the estates to call the married hired men by their surname only, the unmarried men by their first name.

Grugel, the coachman, was in charge of the half dozen horses which were used to pull the buggies. He kept the buggies clean, polished the harnesses and hitched up the horses for the more extensive trips. He also drove to the train station to pick up guests or to take them back. There were days when he needed to make this trip as often as five times. Grugel is reported to have said, "If I would have been in charge of the horses when the train accident occurred, it would not have happened. I would have watched the crossing myself!" I don't know why he moved away but he was replaced by

Franz Kollikowski, who later became the chauffeur when the automobile replaced the horse and buggy.

Another member of the permanent farm staff was *Kollikowski*, father of Franz, the coachman. The senior Kollikowski was in charge of the tools, the threshing machine, the flour mill and other equipment. He had his own working shed and we liked to spend a lot of time with him. He was a wise and highly respected person. I still remember a number of his sayings, some of which are not easy to translate from German to English. His wife was a wise person too. She was the most peaceful in the group of seven women who lived together in the compound of houses at the entrance to the farm.

Exnowsky was another of our workers who later changed his name to Exner when, after 1933, many deleted the "sky" at the end of their names to remove the reminder of their Polish background. Exner was a very capable mechanic. He looked after the tractors and other machinery. We children did not like him very much. His wife was friendly, but we think he was the only one who later was an informer to the Nazi authorities about the activities of the group of people living in our area.

Mutz was the farm foreman. He rang the yard bell for breakfast after the morning chores were done and again at noontime. Mutz was so punctual, we could set the clock according to him. During seeding time he controlled the steering handle of the seed drill and took great pride in making the rows perfectly straight, even when the field was half a kilometre long. He was highly respected by all. We considered him as Vati's partner in managing the farm.

Zett was in charge of feeding the horses and pigs. We had six horses of a lighter breed, which were used for riding and for pulling the buggies. For work on the field we had about 20 heavier draft animals. They were not capable of doing strenuous field work until they were about two-and-a-half years old, so we always had about 14 to 16 young horses around. Besides the regular horses, we always had two ponies for the wagon which we used in summertime to drive to the field to do the milking early in the morning and in the afternoon. The milk was transported to the village of Reichfelde, where the local cooperative produced butter and cheese for market.

The pig barn, which lay adjacent to the stable and had room for up to 120 pigs, was also Zett's responsibility. In the feeding area for hogs was a steam room (*Dämpfanlage*) where potatoes, the main source of food for the hogs, were cooked with hot steam.

Zett was not easy to deal with. When he left our employ he had a difficult time finding a new position. It was well known in the area that people who had worked for my father usually had been spoiled, and often other farmers did not want to hire them.

The *von Almens* from Switzerland were in charge of handling the cattle. Father von Almen was the head herdsman (*Oberschweitzer*). He had to supply his own helpers to handle all the milking, cleaning and feeding so he usually had at least two of his sons working with him.

Funk, the bricklayer (*Mauermeister*), was another special person who often worked on the estate. Our father had a habit of wanting to rearrange things in the various farm buildings, so Meister Funk spent a large proportion of his working time on our farm. He chewed tobacco, smiled a lot, was always ready to share an unexpected joke with young or old, and he had a genuine love for us Bartel children. We could never understand though how his trousers were able to stay in place when the belt holding them up was situated underneath his rotund mid-section!

Each of the permanent men on the farm had a specific area of responsibility, but we also had seasonal workers, sometimes up to 20 of them, who came in spring and stayed until harvest time. Until 1933, they were Polish people who had been hired by a contractor called an *Unternehmer*. He and his wife were in charge of cooking for the group. They all lived in one building which had separate rooms for the men and the women, as well as a few small rooms for couples.

The same man was in charge of our seasonal workers for most of the years we were at Reichfelde, but after 1933 the German Government no longer allowed the hiring of Polish people. This action was an attempt to reduce unemployment among Germans. Usually the relationship between our local farm workers and the seasonal group was good, but even in this situation certain social boundaries were evident.

10. The Farmer as Manager

The management and supervision of the operation in Reichfelde was naturally the farm owner's obligation. He was looked upon as a patriarch by the families living on the farm. Not much work was expected of him, but running the farm operation in an efficient way was a challenge which required the strongest managerial skills.

Higher production was achieved only by rotation of crops and the use of manure from the farm animals. When I was young, the use of tractors, commercial fertilizers and chemical weed control were just in their beginning stages.

Vati was an outstanding breeder of Holstein-Frisian cattle. However, in his goal to be a leader in many areas of farming, he sometimes overestimated the potential financial returns. He invested heavily in improvements to the buildings and in buying the breeding bulls required to improve his herd. That latter expense brought great returns later when Hitler took power and the situation in farming improved, but at the time of their purchase, in 1932-33, Vati's operation was in financial difficulty. Nevertheless, even in those days, he was always willing to help people in need. When there were marriage difficulties, for example, even the farm workers would come to Vati to settle the controversy. He was a highly respected person and a wonderful father.

11. Caught in the System

The class system was still a major influence at that time. It was accepted by all of society, even by our farm labourers. Our status as farmer's sons changed when we completed high school. From that day on I was no longer addressed as Siegfried but as *junger Herr* (young master), and the German form of address "Du" became the formal "Sie." These changes were sometimes fraught with difficulties, especially in our relationship to friends in our own age group. For years we had played together as equals—Christian von Almen, Heinrich Zett and Ernst Mutz were my good friends—and now we had to adjust to a change in position and to the unwritten rules of a class system. When Vati was absent from the farm and there were difficulties between couples or workers, the *Junge Herr* was responsible for settling these disputes.

The family's social life was defined within class boundaries. Even though the boys played with some of the farm workers' children, that hardly applied to our sisters. It would have been almost unthinkable for them to go outside the boundaries of their class to find a marriage partner. Within the Mennonite church it was an exception for someone to marry a non-Mennonite. Marriage partners coming from non-Mennonite backgrounds had to join the Mennonite church if they wanted to be married in that church by a Mennonite minister.

Yet boundaries in the sexual area were not always as clearly observed. Some well-known owners of smaller or larger farms used their superior positions to develop sexual relationships outside their marriages with members of the working class. That was true in the middle and upper classes, the elite, but also among Mennonites.

These elite were the owners and families who had lived on their estates for generations. This group felt superior to my father: *they* were involved in politics; *their* sons were candidates for leadership in the army. I clearly remember the derogatory remarks made about Vati. Such displays of arrogance by this class toward every Mennonite was an unspoken reality.

There were also two groups within the West Prussian Mennonite family. One cluster had served in non-combatant units in World War I; the other had taken up arms. Vati had been exempt from service because of a heart condition, but all the close relatives on both his and Mutti's side had served in Red Cross units. I will never forget the disparaging remarks made about Vati at that time. Mennonites were often accused of building up their farms and becoming rich during wartime while the rest were serving their country in the military.

12. Participation in Church Life

Church was always a very important part of life for our family. My parents had established a group of evangelically oriented young people within our Thiensdorf-Rosengart congregation. Since officially the church did not support—it merely tolerated—this work, Vati organized the youth ministry part of the church on his own terms and on his own time. He made arrangements with a choir director to lead the group in singing. These rehearsals, as well as Bible study sessions, which my father usually led, were held every second Saturday evening.

It is hard to believe how people sacrificed their time to serve in that way. Herr Ludwigkeit, a non-Mennonite, was our choir conductor for many years. He drove his beautiful horse and buggy team for an hour and a half to get to our farm. Then we took our larger buggy with two horses and drove to Rosengart, which took another hour and a half. Two weeks later we made a similar sojourn to Thiensdorf, which took two hours one way. Sometimes, Herr Ludwigkeit spent nearly seven hours away from home in one evening—and without pay. It was an example of dedication in service.

This youth group (*Jugendbund*) was where I had my really close friends and where I first became aware of Erna Siebert. She was the beautiful girl with the high soprano voice. The highlight for us each year was Vati's birthday when all the young people came to Reichfelde for the celebration. Vati was not only the young people's leader; he was also the counsellor and spiritual mentor for many of them. Once a year the young people from all the Mennonite churches in West Prussia and Poland met in Stegen, a resort on the Baltic Sea in the free state of Danzig. That location was chosen to give the churches in Poland the opportunity to participate along with the congregations of West Prussia.

Due to Vati's involvement with the young people, he was invited to the lay ministers' gatherings. Among that group he was considered a "second-class citizen." Because he was not officially elected as a lay minister, he could not stand behind the pulpit, even when he spoke at youth gatherings. I recall how bitter I was toward the church even then when I saw my father standing *beside* the pulpit when he preached.

Not all the sons and daughters of the lay ministers took part in our cluster. Rather, the *Jugendbund* consisted of members of families with strong pietistic orientation. The way of discipleship—following Jesus as Lord and Saviour—was emphasized clearly. However, even those who did not participate in our group all took part in the preparation classes for baptism. Baptism, which took place each year at Pentecost, was not an act of obedience to God for all of them. For some it was merely a ceremony to observe at the age of 14 or 15. Since young people in the Lutheran Church were confirmed at that age, it became customary for some Mennonite youth to be baptized. That is, they became church members in their early teens, but many never took an active part in church life.

13. Testing My Faith

Often the age period from 16 to 20 is a time for establishing values and finding direction for life. Like everyone in our family, I had accepted the religious values of my parents. But times of testing always remain part of the religious journey. I vividly remember one such experience.

One morning, while I was doing my managerial duties on the farm, I had a disagreement with one of the workers. In my frustration I rebuked him, apparently with some unacceptable words. I didn't notice that my father was standing in the doorway of the barn. He was quiet until all the workers had left for their assignments, then he said to me: "So bist Du mein Sohn nicht!" (No son of mine will act in that way!) That was all he said, but his words affected me deeply.

I went into the garden. I still remember the place between the two hedges of evergreens where I knelt down and, with tears in my eyes and with Vati's words still ringing in my ears, I prayed to the Lord for forgiveness. I pledged my desire to do God's will in my relationship to the Lord and to the people around me. That moment was crucial in my decision to follow Christ. Vati never mentioned the incident again, but from then on—and I think for my whole life—I have treated workers more as equals.

Another way of examining my faith was by observing the people close to me. I had serious problems relating to two of my uncles. As a critical teenager I compared them to my father and came up with very different conclusions. Vati was very close to Uncle Otto, his only brother and an elected lay minister in the church. Their kinship ties and their common bond in farming were enhanced by their spiritual closeness in an evangelical interpretation of the gospel and their relationship within the ministerial council meetings. However, I overheard Uncle Otto's occasional cynical remarks about Vati's aptitude for farming. I could not tolerate such comments, nor did I appreciate the way Uncle Otto treated his younger children. When Vati asked me to manage the farm in Grunau for a while in summer 1937, at first I refused. I did not want to have anything to do with Uncle Otto. But Vati insisted and made the decision for me. My relationship to my uncle did improve and, during and after the war, it was very personal and warm. In many ways he later became the family patriarch.

The relationship to Uncle Gustav Andres (Mutti's cousin) was very different. He was a caring family man but that did not carry over to his relationship with all his neighbours. I remember one special incident. We were on one of our visits with all the usual families at the Andres' place when the neighbour Wilhelm Beuttel came to the yard on horseback. Wilhelm was usually dressed very flamboyantly. He rode a white horse and often wore a purple cape. On that occasion he asked for Uncle Gustav and when he came to the front door Wilhelm reprimanded him in a loud voice. Apparently there was a disagreement about the hiring of seasonal workers. We boys were standing in the barn behind the doors, listening. Having delivered his message, Wilhelm Beuttel mounted his horse and galloped from the yard, his purple cape flying behind him.

Why am I writing about these incidents concerning my uncles? As a young man I sometimes questioned the value of Christianity and measured it against the behaviour of people I knew. Naturally, close relatives were the first ones I observed. I am thankful that in this critical teenager's evaluations of Christianity, the positive example of my father was overwhelmingly convincing.

14. Establishing Credentials

The school I attended went only to Grade 10. Ours was the first class which was to have the opportunity to continue on to Grade 13, the university entrance requirement. For reasons not known to me, this upgrading did not materialize. So in 1931 I graduated with a Grade 11 education. I was the only member of the class who failed the final English exam. My teacher, Dr. Stanull, asked if I wanted to take an oral exam to improve my mark. Since I had good marks in the other subjects and didn't need a passing mark in English, I decided not take him up on his offer. I told him that I was planning to be a farmer and didn't think I'd need English to communicate with the cows!

When my formal education came to an end that spring, I joined farm life in Reichfelde. First, I had to get some experience in practical farm work but I never had to cope with an employer-employee relationship. My brother Hans was the farm manager, so during the first year I was a "go-between" person. Later, when Hans went to agriculture college in Elbing, I became farm manager.

In the late 1920s and early 1930s the financial situation for farmers became more and more critical. Vati was not able to pay all his debts, yet he still continued to be helpful to others. I was aware that Vati had lost money in business dealings with relatives and had his own financial problems and couldn't understand why he would keep on helping relatives and friends. For example, in 1927 he and Erna's uncle, Benno Friesen of Altfelde, paid for the David Rempel family to immigrate to Canada.

In spite of financial difficulties on the farm, Vati built up his dairy herd as a breeder. He had an exceptional eye for improving a herd. Muttchen did not share his special interest. Sometimes Vati would return home after two or three days at one of the important cattle shows in Königsberg and would go to the barn to review some of his new ideas for herd improvements before going into the house to greet mother.

On one occasion he was at an auction of selected Holstein Frisian sires in Königsberg when he saw a bull which he thought he simply must have. He bought it on the spot, but without knowing how he would pay for it. When he came home he phoned his brother Otto in Grunau, as he often did, and told him the story. Uncle Otto had always been more prosperous than Vati, thus financially more secure.

Uncle Otto said, "Heinrich, you did something unwise, but I will not leave you in the lurch." So Uncle Otto paid half the price and Leonard, the special bull who sired prize-winning animals, went to Grunau after being used in Reichfelde for two years.

The farmers' struggle to retain and operate their farms came to an end in 1933 when Hitler came to power. One of his first orders was that no farmer would lose his farm for financial reasons. The plan he introduced for debt regulation was drastic and clearly oriented toward farmers. A government-appointed commission was to visit each farm which was in financial difficulty, review the quality of the operation, list all the debts, then establish a reasonable payment plan. That portion of the debt which the farmer could not carry was wiped out by law.

Some negative consequences resulted from this action. Many retired farmers lost their savings. In other cases it benefitted farmers who had spent foolishly or who had acted irresponsibly. Erna's father, who had not borrowed money for farm improvements, felt punished for not making debts. For Vati this action brought great relief.

I remember the day I had to accompany this government commission to look at the fields and examine the quality of farming in Reichfelde. On the way to the village where we had a large pasture, we drove past Uncle Gustav Andres' farm.

One of the committee members asked me, "Why don't you marry one of the Andres' girls; then you would not need the *Umschuldung*" (the name for the process explained above). Such a thing had never entered my thoughts in spite of our close and friendly relationship to the Andres' girls. Apparently, the commission members were as much aware of Uncle Gustav's financial situation as we all were.

During the mid-1930s the financial situation for farmers improved steadily. The success of selling young Holstein bulls for high prices became almost routine. It was during those years that Vati, on his own initiative, paid off the debts which had already been wiped out by law at the time of *Umschuldung*.

In those years the political climate changed. After two years in power, Hitler and his organizations began nurturing their anti-semitic views. I had read Hitler's *Mein Kampf* and Rosenberg's *Der Mythus des 20 Jahrhunderts*, but nobody really thought at the time that the philosophies expressed in those documents could become government guidelines. On the other hand, those of us who depended on agriculture experienced great improvements. Certainly, the propaganda machine was doing its part.

In the spring of 1936 Hans returned from his farming apprenticeship in South Germany to take over management in Reichfelde again. I moved on to the position of assistant farm manager at Bielefeldt in Blumstein. The farm was situated right on the dike of the Nogat, only half an hour by bicycle from Marienburg. It was a well-managed farm but the owner, who had experienced gas poisoning in World War I and as a consequence had epileptic seizures, needed help. I enjoyed working for him. As a farmer he was known for breeding and raising wonderful horses, and I certainly enjoyed riding them. The only problem was that he sometimes became so excited and angry that he had difficulty controlling himself. In such situations he sometimes threw his hat to the ground and trampled on it to show his rage.

15. Foretaste of the Future

During that time I dated Erna more often. On weekends I rode my bicycle approximately 80 kilometres to see her.

In autumn of 1936 I joined the *Reichsarbeitsdienst* (RAD), a military-type training program but without arms. A spade (*Spaten*) as shiny as a mirror became the organization's symbol of unity. The RAD was a method of reducing unemployment. One of our work programs was digging ditches by hand. I must have shown some leadership qualifications because I was the only one who advanced a position after three months of service. Not many people had a driver's license at that time. It became apparent that the medical doctor in charge of the camp was an alcoholic and was not allowed to drive, so I became his chauffeur. It was a good position, especially since it was not controlled by the unit. The doctor sometimes allowed me to use the car to go home to Reichfelde. During my time in the *Arbeitsdienst* I developed into one of the best long distant runners in the unit. Needless to say, we had a lot of time for training. When we won a competition we received extra holidays.

The food at RAD left something to be desired and certainly did not measure up to home cooking. One Sunday at home apparently I had eaten too much. In the afternoon, while visiting relatives in Oberkerbswalde where Erna was working for her sister Liesbeth, I developed a terrible stomach cramp. The doctor had to come and I was not able to return to my unit until the next day. During that short period of recuperation I had excellent care from my sweetheart.

My six-month service with RAD was a wonderful experience. During my time there, Erna had gone to South Germany to get a six-month experience in running a household at the Musselmanns in Hygstetten. When she left, I accompanied her to the train station in Marienburg with a bouquet of roses.

I missed her so much that, when my service ended in spring 1937, I went to visit her. I also went to see my sister Ruth who was working in Hirschegg, Austria. For the rest of that summer I managed the farm for Uncle Otto in Grunau.

On November 3, 1937, I joined the army.

II

War Is Hell

"The glorification of war is the greatest lie in the history of [humankind]. I confess without shame that I am tired and sick of war. Its glory is all moonshine. It is only those who have neither heard a shot or heard the shrieks and groans of the wounded who cry for more blood, more vengeance, more desolation. . . . War is hell!"
General William T. Sherman
August 11, 1880

16. Joining the Army

Although Mennonites had come to Poland in 1530, they were brought under the Prussian crown only in 1771 with the first partition of Poland. In 1774 they were informed that, in lieu of military service, they would have to pay 5,000 taler annually to support the military academy in Kulm. In addition, further acquisition of land was prohibited since military obligations were tied to the land. As a result, a large group of Mennonites moved to Russia in 1787.

However, our forebears stayed in Prussia. Although a Prussian edict in 1867 abolished military exemption, service as non-combatants remained an option. During World War I many of our parents' generation served in such units. Others, however, fully accepted the challenge as German citizens to serve with the army. When Hitler introduced the universal obligation to bear arms (*Allgemeine Wehrpflicht*) on March 16, 1935, the position of nonresistance for Mennonites in Germany virtually came to an end.

By the time I enlisted in 1937, the question of serving in the army was no longer an issue for Mennonites in Prussia. I was 22 years old. When I volunteered, I was deeply convinced that doing my duty in the army was what the Lord expected of me—and had not the slightest conscience pangs about doing so. How could I have predicted that later in life I would change to become a pacifist? By volunteering I could select the unit in which I wanted to serve. Besides that, my best friend and cousin, Hans-Peter Bartel of Grunau, had served two years in Infantry Regiment 45 in Marienburg. If he brought in volunteers he could get extra holidays. That is why his brother Horst and I signed up with Company 13 of Infantry Reserve 45. It was the only unit in a regiment of approximately 3,000 men which was fully equipped with horses and vehicles. The horses were used to pull the unit's six 7.5-centimetre and two 15-centimetre cannons.

Hans-Peter had become a candidate for officer in the Infantry Reserve, so he continued into his third year of training for that role. When Horst and I joined the unit in 1937, Hans-Peter's good leadership had already established the Bartel name. Horst and I were assigned to the same room where we shared a bunk bed. In the unit of about 140 men, Hans-Peter was not our trainer, but we had frequent contact with him and spent many relaxed hours in his private room.

During my first week of service, two incidents had an impact on my place in the unit. On one occasion all the recruits were assembled for athletic competitions. Sergeant Major (*Hauptfeldwebel*) Thams was in charge of the event. Our superiors wore sports attire, just like the rest of us, so we weren't able to recognize them during those first days of training. They had selected two recruits for a boxing match. I still remember their names. Schachtschneider was over two metres tall and weighed approximately 110 kilograms. His opponent was Kortzinjewski, a tailor by vocation. He weighed about 50 kilograms and was the weakest recruit in the unit.

Schachtschneider knocked down the undersized Kortzinjewski with one punch on the nose. When K. tried to get up, his large opponent knocked him down again with what seemed like a fairly gentle punch. Most of the soldiers roared with laughter at the mismatch. Angered by this obviously unfair contest I made a remark to that effect to the man standing beside me. I didn't know until later that his name was Klawitter and that he was one of the most brutal training officers in the regiment.

He pushed me into the boxing ring and told Thams, the training officer in charge, what I had said. The officer responded angrily and, using abusive language, ordered me to have a boxing match with the best boxer on the training staff. I had never been in a boxing ring before. I do not recall if I prayed when I put on the boxing gloves, but I felt deeply outraged by what was happening. The outcome was quick and decisive. Without sustaining a single blow myself, I knocked out my opponent with the first punch. There was silence all around.

Shortly thereafter—I don't remember if it was the same day or the day after the boxing match—the whole unit had to run five kilometres as part of its training exercises. Since I had competed in long-distance running in my recent service program, I had an advantage over the majority of the recruits. I finished in first place. As a result of my boxing and racing achievements during those first few days of training, I earned a special status among both my fellow recruits and my superiors.

The tradition of *being different* had already been established by Hans-Peter before we enlisted. As is the case in most armies around the world, drinking alcohol was considered a sign of belonging. The tendency among soldiers was to get everyone to conform. The commander of our unit, Captain Fischer, was an alcoholic who often drank so heavily that he was not able to walk properly. When other training officers tried to persuade us, sometimes quite forcefully, to join them in their partying and drinking, Captain Fischer always defended us, even though he might be half drunk himself.

One day I heard him say, "Let the Bartels be the way they are. I only wish I could be as determined as they are."

After completing my six months of basic training, I was selected as the only one from the November 1937 group of recruits to become an officer candidate in the Reserves. So I advanced to the position of lance corporal (*Gefreiter*). At that same time the unit was preparing to participate in its first field manoeuvres. One morning, when the entire Company was lined up, the Sergeant Major asked if any of the recruits could ride a horse well enough to ride in the manoeuvres. I volunteered and was ordered to go to the stable and report to Sergeant Breitenbach, the senior riding instructor. Everyone thought I was crazy. No one in the army ever admitted that they had any skills. Those who did were immediately put to the test.

When I reported to the senior riding instructor he laughed at me and said, "Here's a horse for you. Her name is Rosi. The man who tried to ride her yesterday is still in the hospital. Ride her and see what you can do."

Rosi was a beautiful horse. When I got into the saddle, all the trainers moved back some distance, waiting to see what would happen. But Rosi and I took a shine to each other immediately. Since I had experience on the farm with breaking in horses, within half an hour I had her doing anything that was expected of her. I ended up riding that beautiful horse Rosi during the manoeuvres. Later she became the riding horse for the commander of the Regiment. Because of my success with Rosi who was at the training stage, the following week I was assigned to the training class for young horses as one of an "elite selection of riders." Normally such assignments were given only to soldiers with three or four years of training.

17. Engagement midst Clouds of War

During basic training in the winter of 1937-38, none of the recruits got much time off. My holidays were at Christmas and, because every soldier got one free trip a year on the German public train system, I took that trip to Hirschegg to visit my friend Erna Siebert, or Ernusch, as I called her. She was working at a holiday resort owned by Gertrud Kröker, my brother Hans's sister-in-law.

The Walserthal was part of Austria, but accessible only via Oberstdorf on the German side. As a German soldier I was not allowed to cross the border so, before boarding the bus in Oberstdorf, I changed into civilian clothes. That was strictly forbidden, but I did it anyway. My sister Ruth was also working at Hirschegg. I had an enjoyable time there in spite of the fact that Ernusch got little time off from work to be with us. If we would have been publicly engaged it might have been different. As it was I joined other resort guests on day tours into the Austrian Alps. But the evenings were ours.

Ernusch returned home in the spring of 1938 and, on June 5, we announced our engagement. She turned 19 that month; I was 23. We had been close friends for a number of years and neither of us had been involved in other serious relationships, even though we had a large circle of friends. We had shared our love for each other through many letters. Our plans now were for me to complete two years of service in the army. Then Vati would divide Reichfelde into two farms. With that in mind, a duplex for farm workers had been built in 1937.

In spring 1938, after my first promotion to lance corporal, I was made responsible for the new recruits. One man in this unit named Helling was mentally disturbed. The army doctors had permitted him to start his training but if he did not prove himself, he would be released from the army as one who was "incapable of serving." When Helling had been with us for several weeks, I was summoned into the office of Captain Fischer, the commander of our Company.

He explained Helling's situation, showed me his medical files, then said, "Bartel, I am assigning this man to your room with other recruits so that you can observe him continuously. In three weeks I want a report from you. I will accept your judgement. If you say he is unable to serve for psychological reasons, we will release him regardless of what the doctors say." After only two weeks I went to Captain Fischer's office and reported that Helling was definitely mentally disturbed. A few days later he was released.

In fall of 1938 I became an intermediate officer (*Unteroffizier*), the next step up the ladder toward becoming an officer. That turned out to be the most enjoyable period during my service in the army, and for more than one reason. First, the financial situation of our family's farm had improved considerably. Secondly, Vati had bought a new

*Our engagement in
June 1938*

BMW car, which allowed me to take the older BMW to the army
compound. That meant I could visit my sweetheart more often. The
regulations of an intermediate officer made it possible for me to move
more freely outside the compound.

By that time Hitler had aggressively built up his army and had
absorbed Austria and Sudetenland (part of Czechoslovakia) into
Germany. An area in Sudetenland was known worldwide for raising
beautiful Arabian horses many of which were brought to our unit.
Based on my past experience, I was assigned to evaluate them for their
suitability as riding horses in the army.

As 1939 began, the clouds of war became more and more apparent
on the horizon. How was it possible that, after only 20 years,
countries were again preparing for war? Immediately after World
War I, Germany had been in economic chaos. Six million people were

unemployed. The threat of communism forced people to look for alternatives, which for many became the NSDAP (*National Sozialistische Deutsche Arbeiter Partei)*, the official name of the Nazi party.

By the time Adolf Hitler became Chancellor of Germany in 1933, the country was ready for strong, dictatorial leadership. To deal with the unemployed he introduced RAD (*Reichsarbeitsdienst)* and universal military training. The building of a modern freeway (*Reichsautobahn)* brought millions of unemployed back to work. In only six years he brought Germany from the ruinous aftermath of World War I to a highly productive industrial capability.

Although individual freedom became more and more curtailed through the secret police, the Gestapo *(Geheime Staats Polizei)*, the propaganda machine under Joseph Goebbels prepared the population for the *necessity* of dealing with Poland. Hitler established a strong army which helped nurture the patriotic feelings toward the nation.

On the foreign front Hitler also made a name for himself. By absorbing Austria, later Sudetenland (part of Czechoslovakia) into Germany, by 1938 he had become the undisputed master of central Europe. Influenced by his achievements in foreign affairs, Hitler tightened his grip by quelling the slightest opposition or criticism within Germany. Not only was he a master at influencing public opinion, he also was obsessed with his dream of controlling central Europe and consumed by his sense of power. Could no one stop this dictator?

Hindsight always provides easy answers, especially for people who did not walk in our shoes and did not know the reality of the hour. Thousands who tried to change the country's path were executed in gas chambers, hanged or shot. Many of us did what we considered to be our *duty* to our country and entered the trenches during the war. We did not know what was going on behind the front lines or, as in my case, discovered little by little what was actually happening, but were not able to do anything about it except continue to be obedient cogs in the huge war machine.

In summer 1939, when the outbreak of war was imminent, our field manoeuvres took on the character of actual war exercises. In the meantime I had advanced to the level of sergeant major (*Feldwebel)*, the last position before becoming an officer. I was assigned to Unit 4, which had 15-centimetre grenades, the only two such cannons within an Infantry Regiment. My cousin, Hans-Peter, was in charge of Unit 1 and his brother Horst was assigned to Unit 2. So all three of us were in the same Company but in different units.

The 21st Infantry Division, with Regiments 3, 24 and 45, was stationed in the Marienburg-Marienwerder (Prussian Eylau) area where the war exercises were held. On August 31, 1939, the day before the Second World War began, we were stationed in the woods close to the Goertz family farm. The Goertz's were friends of Vati and Uncle Otto.

As an officer, Hans-Peter had more knowledge about what was really going on and had informed his father about our whereabouts. During the afternoon of what turned out to be the last day of peace, Vati, Ernusch, Uncle Otto and Hans-Peter's wife, Lena, came to the Goertz farm for afternoon coffee. Hans-Peter took Horst and me along. I remember sitting in that garden with coffee and cake, totally unaware that the war would start the very next morning. We did not want to believe that the clouds of war would descend so soon. But an ominous sense of reality overshadowed our outward display of optimism when we embraced in an emotional farewell.

18. The War Begins

On September 1, 1939, at 4:45 in the morning, Germany attacked Poland. The Second World War had begun.

The same evening as I visited with my father and my fiancée at our friend's farm near Marienwerder, we took up our positions for an early morning attack on Poland. As a newly named sergeant major, I took charge of a unit, the one with the 15-centimetre grenades in which I had received my basic training. Those two artillery cannons, pulled by six horses, were the heaviest armaments within an Infantry Regiment and had a range of 7,500 metres.

The time of the attack was set for 4:45 a.m. From our position we could see the front trenches of the Polish Army on the other side of the border. The order was to cover those trenches for a short time until our other infantry units would storm the hill.

It was the responsibility of a small group from our unit to be with the soldiers immediately behind the front lines and to direct the fire. Orders were given via the wireless or telephone to the artillery cannons, which usually were positioned 500 to 1,000 metres behind the lines. Often the men firing the cannons could not see the enemy and waited for their orders from the man in charge of conducting the fire. That first morning of the Second World War it was my responsibility to give the orders to the artillerymen.

When we stormed the hill at which I had directed the fire, we came upon a blonde young man lying outside the trench. He had been bandaged up by his comrades but, because of their hasty retreat, the Polish soldiers had not been able to take him along.

I made my way to him, looked into his face and—to this day, I do not know why—I asked him: "Sind Sie ein Pole?" (Are you Polish?)

I was shocked when he answered in my own German dialect, "Nein, ich bin Evangelisch" (No, I am a Lutheran). The majority of Polish citizens were Catholic, but the German minority in that country consisted mostly of Mennonites and Lutherans. When he answered me in my mother tongue my thoughts immediately flashed to my cousin, Walter Schroeder, who was serving in the Polish Army.

After I had directed the artillery fire at the hill ahead of us, something within me kept saying: "I could have killed my own cousin." That thought has never left me. Even now, 50 years later, as I write down this incident, the memory is so vivid that it could have happened yesterday.

Two days later our regiment was positioned outside of Graudenz, the city where Vati went to school. The highest point of the city was the steeple of the garrison church. It was assumed that the observers who were directing the Polish artillery attack were located in the apex of the steeple. Our unit received the order to destroy it. But since the target was not visible, we could only achieve our goal by following measurements on the map. I don't know if we succeeded in hitting our mark, but the thought has come back to me again and again, "You, as a born-again Christian, were conducting the fire to destroy a church!" The city of Graudenz was turned over to our Commander, Colonel V. Behr, on September 4.

After that encounter, the order came for our Division to be transported to Johannesburg with instructions to attack the Polish units in the area of Bialystock. There we met the Russian units which had occupied the eastern part of Poland. That is when the war with Poland came to an end.

Our unit experienced a wonderful welcome on our return to the garrison, Marienburg. What a joy it was to greet loved ones again. But not everyone could say that. From our home church, Hans Cornelsen, father of two, a friend of many of us, had died during the first day of fighting. Many others whom we did not know personally had suffered the same fate.

19. War Academy----Wedding at Christmas

After we returned to Marienburg, I received orders to attend the War Academy in Berlin for four months of further preparation as an officer in the Reserve. Two days after we attacked Poland, its allies, France and Great Britain, declared war on Germany. That response was a clear indication that the fighting would not end quickly. Earlier, Erna and I had thought we would wait with our wedding until after the war. But this new development caused us to change our marriage plans. Since I would be getting a brief, five-day leave during the Christmas season, we decided on a December 23rd wedding.

As an officer candidate in the Army, I had to get permission from my commander's office to get married. Since I still belonged to my active unit, which in the meantime had been relocated to the western front toward France, I applied to them for authorization. However, their office took the position that, since I was attending the War Academy, I belonged to the units stationed at home.

When I arrived at Ernusch's parents in Markushof on December 20, just three days before the wedding, I still had not received permission from either of the Army offices to which I had applied. So, on December 21, I took the train to Braunsberg, where our unit's home office was located and applied again. I also phoned my cousin and close friend, Hans-Peter Bartel, since he was an experienced officer in our field unit and might have some pull. On December 22 I received permission by telegram from both offices.

Of course we wanted to have our entire family circle present at the celebration. That hope faded as we approached the wedding date. Alfred, Erna's brother, was in a hospital in Warsaw with a very serious ear infection. The two brothers-in-law in our Bartel family did not receive Christmas holidays from their army units so Magdalena and Gertraut were there without their husbands. Muttchen also was not able to be with us that day. For a number of years she had been afflicted with a rare disease which affected her muscles and gave her serious headaches. All my brothers and sisters were present, but for only about three hours. It was the last time we were all together.

As was the custom at weddings in Germany, the legal ceremony before a government official took place in the forenoon. Two witnesses were present, my brother Hans and our brother-in-law Ernst Quapp. During Hitler's regime, couples were discouraged from having church weddings, so the official service was conducted much more as a ceremonial event. The official representative of the state (*Standesbeamte*), Herr Genzel, made the ritual so solemn and formal that Ernst and I had a hard time suppressing our laughter.

The church ceremony was at the Mennonite meeting house in Thiensdorf. That was the church where Erna had been baptized. Her father, a lay minister, married us. The text we had chosen was, "For no other foundation can any one lay than that which is laid, which is Jesus Christ" (1 Corinthians 3:11).

How difficult it must have been for Emil Siebert, a pacifist Mennonite preacher, to perform the marriage of his youngest daughter, his "Puppelein" (little doll), to a man standing before him wearing an army uniform, a sergeant with the traditional sword hanging at his side—and all of that in a Mennonite church. The fact that we had chosen Menno Simon's motto as a wedding text must have added to the incongruity of the situation.

I wish now that I had a copy of his meditation. At the time I accepted his sermon as coming from a man who did not understand the greatness of the era in which we were living. In reality, however, he was the only one in our circle of relatives who was uncompromising in his interpretation of scripture and history. The rest of us sided with the system.

The wedding reception was held at the home of Ernusch's parents in Markushof, where a wonderful banquet was prepared. It was customary to hire an experienced female kitchen chef (*Kochfrau*) to be in charge of the meal with neighbours assisting in the preparations. Approximately 60 guests were invited to the reception. The neighbours who helped were invited to a thank you dinner at a later date.

Because Muttchen could not be at the wedding, Ernusch and I took the one-and-a-half-hour coach trip from Markushof to Reichfelde. It gave us some time to reflect on our future. Muttchen was very sick that day so we spent only a short time with her. As we began our married journey together, we knelt for prayer in the *Hofzimmer* (the upstairs guest bedroom with a view of the farm buildings) and asked the Lord for his blessing and guidance in our married life. A few days later I returned to Berlin to finish my time at the War Academy. Erna was able to visit me twice in Berlin before I had to go back to my field unit.

The training program at the Academy was very professional with few political overtones. It focused on planning strategies and developing decision-making skills. Graduation at the Academy, at which Hitler gave the address, concluded with my advancement to the rank

At our wedding on December 23, 1939, with Erna's family (standing, from left): Elfriede Pauls, Hermann Pauls, the bride, Ernst Bartel, the groom, Liesbeth Bartel, Trudchen Siebert, Ernst Quapp, Hildegard Quapp; (seated, from left): Emil Siebert, Klara Siebert with Gertraut Siebert; (sitting on floor): Alice, Erika and Hanna Quapp.

At our wedding with my family (standing, from left): Reinhard Bartel, Magdalena Schneiderreit, Heinz-Otto Bartel, Gretel Bartel, Walter Bartel, Rudolf Wiehler, Hanna Bartel, Hans Bartel, Ruth Schröder, Gertraut Hörr; (seated): Heinrich Bartel with Dorothea Schneiderreit, the bridal couple.

of Lieutenant, the first rank as an officer. With that promotion I joined a new level of leadership in the Army. After serving in the Army for only 26 months, I became the superior to the corporals who had trained me when I first joined up. At the time I did not doubt for a moment that I was doing what God wanted of me. How differently I viewed that later on, when I interpreted Jesus' teachings on love—love which is to include the "enemy."

While I had been at the Academy, my field unit, Infantry Division 21, had taken up its position at the confluence of the Rhine and Mosel rivers. After my arrival there I was put in charge of the heavy artillery (*Schwere Infanterie Geschütze*), the same unit in which I had served during the war in Poland.

20. New Life between Battles

I have before me a little book, *Die deutschen Divisionen: 21. Infanterie Division*, which describes the experiences of our Infantry Division. It was written by Hans-Henning Podzun, a fellow officer who became a close friend. He wrote:

> Spring 1940 was sunny and warm. On May 4 our Division received orders to prepare for action. On May 5 we entered Luxembourg, then we marched through Belgium into France to the area of Charlesville-Mezieres. At Rethel our Division became involved in heavy fighting (Podzun, 4-5).

In the battle at Rethel I was wounded for the first time. Although I didn't need to be hospitalized, I still carry a small piece of the grenade which exploded in the trees beside us.

For the German side, the Battle of France consisted mainly of the actions of our motorized detachments. The infantry divisions had a hard time keeping up with those mobile units. For a number of days we had to march 18 to 20 hours a day. On that march I learned that a person can walk and sleep at the same time. The three Bartels, Hans-Peter, Horst and I, sometimes walked together. One night I saw Hans-Peter on the other side of the road. In front of him was a heap of gravel. He walked right into that pile and fell on his hands and knees, waking up with a start.

It was harvest time when the Battle of France came to an end. During a time of war the production of food is of extreme importance. Since I was a trained agriculturist it became my responsibility to oversee harvesting in the area occupied by our Division. That applied primarily to farms where the French owners were absent or where manpower was in short supply. I had special orders from the General to assign army units to assist in the harvesting operation.

During that assignment I had a service car and driver at my disposal, thus was able to see much of the countryside. Sometimes I took Hans-Peter along and we could do some shopping, mainly gifts and material for our wives. Silk, for example, which had not been available in Germany for years was easily obtainable in France.

The harvesting assignment came to an end when our Division was relocated to the Rhine Valley. One Sunday morning I visited the Mennonite church in that area. There, for the first and only time in my life, I heard a sermon delivered by a Mennonite preacher who was wearing the uniform of a German officer. His name was Brother Schnebele. Although I had no qualms about my own participation in the army at that time, I nevertheless found it strange to see an officer *preaching* in a Mennonite church.

On September 17, 1940, our Division was transported by train to our home base in Marienburg. When we arrived we were welcomed by the whole city, especially by our loved ones. In France I had received the Iron Cross Second Class for bravery as well as a medallion for being wounded.

In preparation for an increase of manpower in the army, our Division, numbering approximately 17,000 men, had to give up one regiment to form a new Division. Our Battalion was chosen for that purpose. Those changes resulted in the separation of the three Bartels. Only Horst remained in that unit. Hans-Peter became head of Company 13 in Infantry Regiment 24; I became Second Aide to the Commander of the newly-established 3rd Battalion within Infantry Regiment 45.

Changes in assignment were always accompanied by separation from people to whom one had become very attached. Besides my cousins, one of those was Hans Höpfner, who was in charge of the horses which pulled the cannons and had been trained as a herdsman. He was a few years older than I. Hans had been called into military service shortly before the war and was under my command during the campaigns in Poland and France. We had established close ties and did not know then if we would ever meet again.

The fall and winter months of 1940-41 were spent at our home base in Marienburg, training for the newly established 3rd Battalion. During that time Erna and I had a comfortable apartment in the army barracks. As was the custom for officers in the Army, a private was assigned to me to look after my affairs; another private was in charge of my riding horse. During the time of training in Marienburg one of my responsibilities was to teach officer candidates how to ride horses. In peacetime it was the custom in army units which had horses to organize hunts in autumn. Those few months were the only times when we experienced the comforts of social life in the officer corps. We enjoyed the comradely relationships, some of which lasted a whole lifetime.

During that time Erna became pregnant. On May 18, 1941, our son Siegfried (Bibi) was born. As was customary then, a midwife came to the home to assist in the delivery. Since there were some difficulties, she found it necessary to call the specialist from Elbing. Bibi was three weeks premature. Because of his early arrival I was able to be present at his birth. What a special gift it was for me to be at Erna's bedside in those hours, witnessing the great challenge of a young mother giving birth to her first child. With deep thankfulness to the Lord and in admiration of Ernusch, I knelt in thanksgiving beside her bed.

The military campaigns in Poland and France were behind us, but we could see the menacing clouds of additional battles on the horizon. I had been wounded once. The chances of an infantry officer surviving several major military actions were small. Erna's wish to have "a little Siegfried," in case I would not return from the battlefield, was fulfilled. After that wonderful occasion, I returned to my unit which was already stationed close to the eastern border of Germany. The attack on Russia was only a month away.

The new Commander of the 3rd Battalion was Captain Hufenbach. He was a highly decorated officer and an excellent fighter. But in other respects, such as in his ethical standards and in some of his other attributes, he did not measure up to the rest of the officers I knew.

21. The Beginning of the End

Until then, German operations in Poland and in the West had been straight military actions, fought according to the rules of the Geneva Convention. The well-known British historian Liddell Hart wrote: "One of the surprising features of the Second World War was that the German Army in the field on the whole observed the rules of war better than it did in 1914-18, at any rate in fighting its Western opponents" (Hart, *The Other Side of the Hill*, 29).

That changed at the beginning of the war against the U.S.S.R. when Hitler gave the order on May 14, 1941, that any Soviet Kommissar taken as prisoner-of-war was to be executed on the spot. Kommissars were Communist Party officials who were attached to Russian army units and had more power than the military officers who were in charge of those units. That order, presented to the officers of our Division by word-of-mouth on the eve of our attack on Russia, created a deep sense of discontent among the officers present. Hitler's S.S. units had disregarded Geneva Convention rules before, but the new command created a sensation for the regular army units. The order was later rescinded by Hitler after he learned that Russian soldiers became strengthened in their resolve to fight to the finish rather than allowing themselves to become prisoners-of-war.

During my time in the Army I worked with many officers. Of all of them, Major Hufenbach was the only one who obeyed Hitler's "Kommissar order." With that questionable command hanging heavily on our minds, the attack on Russia began at 3:05 a.m. on June 22. It was Erna's birthday.

Among the German officers leading the invasion were many who knew that this battle could not be won. One of the universal tragedies of war is when military personnel who have promised to obey orders know that a campaign in which they are about to engage will lead to self destruction.

Our regiment became involved in heavy fighting on the third day. I received the Iron Cross First Class for my part in that battle. In fall, a letter from Commander Hufenbach commended me for demonstrating "special bravery at the battle in the woods at Poprudze" as, under heavy enemy fire, I "made contact with our other units, in spite of the fact that the forest was still partly in Russian hands. Making those connections during the battle contributed to the success of the operation," wrote Hufenbach, as he offered his congratulations for the Iron Cross award.

The war dragged on. That summer I met my brother Reinhard for the last time. Very early one morning in late August, I saw one of his superiors beside the road and inquired if he knew where my brother was. He pointed to one of the big transport vehicles. Among the dozen or more men sleeping in their seats, each rolled up in his own blanket, I finally found Reinhard. We talked a little while, embraced, then I departed.

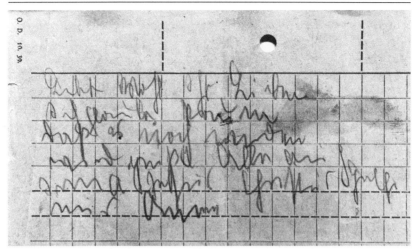

A copy of the note which brother Reinhard wrote just before he died on the battlefield: "Lebt wohl ihr Lieben. Ich glaube kaum dass es noch werden wird. Grüsst allen, auch Irma. Jesus Christus hilft mir. Amen" (Good-bye, my loved ones! I think I will not make it. Greet everyone, including Irma [the girl he loved]. Jesus Christ will be my help. Amen.)

One week later he died in action. He sustained a very serious wound, but was still able to write a short note to the family. The paper on which he wrote his final words was heavily smudged with his blood. "Good-bye, my loved ones! I think I will not make it. Greet everyone, including Irma [the girl he loved]. Jesus Christ will be my help. Amen." We could barely decipher the *Amen*.

In late September the motorcycle on which I was riding was involved in an accident. I was sitting behind the driver who lost control of the vehicle on a sandy path. The main ligament in my right knee was torn in the mishap. I was transported to the army hospital in Elbing. After they put on a cast, I was given a home leave to be with my family. When it was removed I had to travel to the hospital every day for therapy.

In a few weeks I was discharged to my reserve unit in Goldap, the training unit for our field regiment. There I received further treatment. During holidays Erna and our little Bibi were allowed to join me. We had access to a comfortable army apartment during those brief, but very enjoyable, times together.

When I returned to the field I realized how great the losses in our Division had been in the fierce engagements which had taken place on the northern front, especially in October and November: 3,150 dead; 1,030 lost through sickness, 25 percent of those as a result of frost (Podzun, 10). Those battles had taken place on the northeastern portion of the front. On December 20 we commenced a retreat. The first phase of our withdrawal took us to the Wolchow River. The temperature plummeted to minus 43 degrees Celsius.

On December 24 I had an experience which influenced my thoughts on war in a very special way later in my life. It was Christmas Eve and I was walking among the men stationed in the front trenches. It was customary for an officer to spend as much of Christmas as possible with the men under his command. As I circulated among the soldiers I noticed one who was a short distance in front of the line, encroaching on no-man's land between the two opposing entrenchments. He motioned to me to come over to where he was operating a listening device. Frozen ground conducts sound like a wire.

"Listen to this," he said and gave me the earphones. There on that battlefield I heard Christmas carols coming from the trenches of the enemy. As I listened, my thoughts flashed back to Christmas Eve celebrations at Reichfelde when our family would gather in the living room with the farm workers and their families. I recalled the decorated Christmas tree which we children could not see before the celebration. I saw in my mind's eye the table laden with gifts and colourful platters of Christmas goodies. I remembered how we sang carols, then Vati would read the Christmas story and we children would recite poems which we had learned for the occasion.

Now I was hearing Russian soldiers singing about the birth of Christ. Were those enemy fighters also remembering warm family times as they sang? Were they also wondering what "peace on earth" meant during times of war? Later in life I realized, "My pacifism, which I cherish so much today, may have been born at that moment."

In early 1942 the front line was quieter, and I received a three-month study leave to attend an agricultural college in Osnabrück. Our little boy, Bibi, stayed with Grandma Siebert, enabling Erna to join me for that time. That was where we met Wilhelm Wender with whom we developed a close and lasting friendship. He had been an officer in a tank unit and had been seriously wounded.

On April 1 I returned to the reserve unit in Goldap for six weeks before rejoining my field unit. In early summer heavy fighting again broke out. Hans-Henning Podzun described the situation thus: "In summer 1942 the announcement of the German army report mentioned the heavy defence battle along the Wolchow. Stalin personally had ordered the opening of the way to Leningrad" (Podzun, 11).

During that battle I was wounded again. A fragment from a Russian grenade which exploded in some nearby trees hit me in the back close to the spine. It was very difficult to get wounded personnel out of the battle zone. Many seriously injured soldiers who had been fighting in the swamp drowned in the quagmire before help could get to them. I was able to walk toward the Red Cross station on my own, but I became weak and fainted because I had lost a lot of blood. The men working at the station saw me fall in the swamp and picked me up.

I do not know how long I was unconscious. When I woke up I was lying in an army wagon being pulled by four horses. Beside me was my good friend Günter Will, another officer from our regiment. He was wounded more seriously than I. During the trip through the deep mud, lying flat on the floor of the wagon, both of us drifted in and out of consciousness. Finally, we arrived at the waiting Red Cross train during the night, were transferred to one of the cars and given medical attention. The train took us to Riga, where we were hospitalized for more treatment. The hospital was overcrowded and the staff overworked but, because I was in better condition than my friend, I was able to look after him.

Much later Günter Will wrote to me: "I thank you for the two or three extra days you spent in Riga with me before going to your home hospital. It is an unforgettable experience when someone is prepared to watch over another person in this way."

From Riga I was transported to Elbing by air. That was only 20 kilometres from Markushof, our home at that time. The doctors at the hospital decided to leave the piece of steel (two centimetres square) in my back for the time being. They were afraid that an operation would be too risky because the metal was very close to the spine. I recovered quickly and, on September 20, began my duties at the reserve unit in Goldap again, training new recruits. After serving there until Christmas I again received leave to study and to complete my diploma in agriculture, this time in Bramsche. Ernusch and Bibi were able to join me there.

Wilhelm Wender was also at the school, but he was suffering increasingly from the malaria which he had contracted while fighting in Africa. When the time came for writing the final exam, he was sitting beside me. I noticed that he was trying desperately to write something but was unable to do so. After I completed my exam, I didn't hand it in but wrote the exam on his topics which were different than mine. Then I gave it to him to recopy and hand in. I had written two separate papers during that one five-hour sitting, receiving an A on mine and a C on his. I was happy that I could help my sick and suffering friend.

22. My Darkest Hour

In April 1943 I returned to my reserve unit and was immediately transferred to a training camp 150 kilometres behind the front line. That was the area where German occupational units had to deal with both the Russian resistance movement and with the partisan units fighting against the German forces behind the front lines. Those groups were well organized, heavily armed and impossible to control. When our units came into the populated villages, everything appeared to be peaceful. However, many village people were involved in violent actions during the night; some were even participants in the organized resistance movement. Railway tracks were often blown up and nighttime attacks on army barracks and similar acts of resistance happened regularly.

One night I was with my unit of approximately 150 men on a training excursion through the fields. As we left one of the villages we came under heavy machine-gun fire. We were fortunate not to have any casualties. Other units had experienced heavy losses in similar situations.

Our information network had proof that a young man in our village had been the contact person for the partisan units and was informing them about our activities and movements. Receiving that information was the beginning of the darkest hour in my life. After consulting with our security personnel, I, as the commander in charge, gave the order to arrest the man. Then, acting on the information I had received, I gave the order to have him executed. Thinking as I did then, it seemed as if I had no alternative. Little did I know that the guilt and pain of that action would go with me throughout the rest of my life!

It was in mid-1943 that I, as Commander of the German forces in a large area, was invited to a party for high-ranking officers in that region. Some S.S. officers (Hitler's special units) were present as well. The consumption of alcohol during the course of the evening was high, and a number of the people present drank too much. Usually on such occasions my fellow officers were relaxed if I was around.

On the Russian front with my horse after my promotion to the post of Second Assistant (Ordonnanz Offizier) *to the Commander of Infantry Regiment 45.*

They often said, "If we drink too much and if we aren't able to look after ourselves, Siegfried will take care of us."

That evening an S.S. officer who had consumed too much liquor indicated that he wanted to talk to me. He looked to be in his late twenties. His unit had been responsible for mass executions. Never before or after have I talked to someone who had participated in something like that. He started to weep and showed me his hands.

"I have a baby at home," he said, "but these hands will never touch that baby. These hands are full of blood!" A few weeks later he committed suicide.

At about that time, the grenade fragment in my back began to trouble me. It needed to be removed. The surgery was done in my home hospital in Elbing, giving me a short time for home leave and recovery time. Immediately after I returned to my unit, I was transferred back to my original field unit Infantry Regiment 45. I had been there only a short time when I received news of the birth of our son, Gerd, on November 13.

My new post was that of Second Assistant (*Ordonnanz Offizier*) to the Commander of Infantry Regiment 45. Hans-Henning Podzun wrote: "In fall 1943 the 21st Infantry Division had a fairly quiet time in the area of Tschudowo" (Podzun, 14). That "quiet time" enabled me to go home on leave for Christmas to see our baby, Gerd.

On that trip death again came very close, but once more I was spared. My motorcycle driver, Hans Maus, was to take me to the train station. With me in the sidecar, we drove through the woods where we encountered an army unit on the road. I asked Hans to stop so I could check if we would be able to pass them. When I had walked about 20 metres, Hans tried to follow with the motorcycle. The wheel of the sidecar hit a Russian landmine. Hans Maus was thrown into the snowy minefield, heavily wounded. The sidecar in which I had been riding until just minutes before was hanging in hundreds of pieces from the trees around us.

I got Hans Maus out of the minefield, not knowing if there might be other mines deep in the snow. We lifted him on one of the trucks and transported him to a nearby Red Cross station. It became clear that Hans would not survive the serious injuries he had sustained. I left him in care of the Red Cross personnel, but before my departure he asked me for a last wish.

"In my belongings are letters to me from a certain girl," he said. "I do not want those letters to be sent with my belongings to my wife. Please make sure that they are destroyed." I contacted the officer in charge of his unit to pass on Hans's request. Many times since then I have asked myself, "What will be my last thought if I have only a few minutes left to live?"

When I returned to my Regiment, the planned, and often unplanned, retreat of the German Army became a reality. The order to begin the retreat came on January 17, 1944. In early March I was able to visit Ernusch and our two little boys on a short home leave. Later that month and in April our Regiment was involved in heavy fighting, experiencing great losses. Then, with additional personnel arriving, the whole Division had a fairly calm May and June. We even had time for leisure activities. Several riding competitions were organized, one by our Regiment in which 128 riders took part under my leadership.

23. Our Saddest Day

Through the steady exchange of correspondence with Erna I was always kept informed about how she and the boys were faring. Although it was not always possible, I tried to write to her every day during the entire war. I must pay tribute to the Feldpost, the organization which delivered the mail. Sometimes they made seemingly impossible tasks possible.

Erna had written to me that Bibi would need to have surgery for a small internal hernia. I knew that a date had been set for his operation. On July 9 I was called into the office of my friend Klaus von Kursell, the Adjutant.

Looking very solemn, he said, "Siegfried, I have a telegram for you."

My immediate question was, "Did my son die?"

"Yes," he replied.

Erna had taken Bibi to the hospital in Marienburg, where a well-known surgeon was willing to do the operation. After surgery Bibi developed inflammation of the lungs. At that time anaesthetic was administered by inhaling. Apparently, Bibi's lungs had not been cleaned properly with oxygen. The day after the operation Ernusch was called to the hospital because his condition was deteriorating. A blood transfusion from her did not bring improvement. Ernusch was able to stay with him for night. On Sunday morning she went to the chapel in that Catholic hospital where the doctor was playing the organ.

Our three-year-old son Bibi (Siegfried) shortly before he died.

After he had finished the piece, he was called out and accompanied Ernusch to Bibi's bed. Standing beside her he said, "There is nothing more I can do for him."

That Sunday morning Bibi's soul went into eternity. Ernusch knelt down beside the bed, thanking God for his short life. What strength in her spiritual relationship to God, that she was able to pray, "Not my will, but yours be done."

Ernusch was all by herself during that difficult time. The telegram which she sent to me the "normal way" never arrived. She talked to several people to receive their counsel. One was Siegfried Ecker, my close friend and a high ranking officer at the unit in Danzig, who was recuperating there from a serious head wound. Erna phoned him and, contrary to strict military regulations, he sent the telegram about Bibi's death to my unit via the army's telegraph network. I received the message within minutes of its transmission.

Then Erna contacted Stabszahlmeister Ohlendorf, the officer in charge of army vehicles used for maintenance in Marienburg. To save gas, it was impossible to get permission to use a civilian motor vehicle for moving a dead body during wartime. Because of that prohibition it would have been impossible to bury Bibi in our home cemetery.

However, Ohlendorf was willing to supply an army truck to transport the coffin to our Thiensdorf church.

At that time, the front was fairly quiet but a major offensive by the Russian forces was expected any day. For that reason home leaves were forbidden for everyone. After I received the message of Bibi's death, Commander Schwender was granted special permission from the General to give me a one-week home leave to be with Ernusch to bury our firstborn.

The only links to the front at that time were the Red Cross trains and army transports. I was allowed to use one of their trains and was even able to inform Erna of my arrival time in Elbing. The train was not scheduled to stop there but the crew made an exception for me. I still remember the spot at the large, otherwise completely deserted train station where Ernusch was standing when I, the only disembarking person, stepped off the train. When we embraced, our tears were able to flow for the first time since Bibi's death.

Our little boy was lying in a coffin festooned with white lilies when I saw him in the small funeral chapel at the hospital in Marienburg. A three-ton army truck served as the hearse which brought the coffin to the church in Thiensdorf where we buried him.

Bibi had been the darling for many in our family circle, especially for Erna's parents. Grandpa (*Opa*) Siebert took his death very hard, and for his sake Erna could not show her grief openly. A pillar of strength for Ernusch was her mother—that wonderful woman with deep faith and personal strength in a time of grief and suffering.

Gerd, just eight months old, was now our only boy—and what a special gift he was. In spite of the distressing time, Ernusch wished to have a "replacement" for Bibi, the Lord willing. Nine turbulent months later Reinhard Siegfried was born.

When I returned to the front I quickly became aware of the kind of battle our unit had experienced during my absence. Many of my companions were dead; others were wounded. The German Army was in full scale retreat.

We on the front were not affected by an historically significant incident which had taken place in mid-1944. On July 20 some of the high-ranking officers attempted to kill Hitler. He was wounded, although only slightly. The reaction toward the army leadership was devastating. The names of those who were executed after the assassination attempt fill seven pages in the book, *Offiziere gegen Hitler* (Officers Opposed to Hitler, 220-227). The document also included the names of women.

Officers who had been friends of the executed took transfers to front-line units so as to disappear from posts of high command. The soldiers fighting on the front lines were all so preoccupied with trying to survive that they had no time to even think about involvement in a mutiny. Furthermore, those of us fighting on the front lines had little knowledge of the terror which Hitler's S.S. troops and the secret police were wreaking at home.

Toward the end of September the battles became more and more fierce. Podzun commented on that stage of the war:

> September 21, 1944, was the beginning of the darkest day for the 21st Division. Major Meiritz died. Major Lehmann and most of the battalion's commanders were wounded. Major Schaper, leader of the 3rd Regiment, died; and on September 22, Colonel Schwender died (Podzun, 19).

Schwender was my Commander. The battles which followed brought the front line into German territory. That was a clear indication that we were losing the war.

I cannot remember any more how I received the information that my brother Hans was in the same war zone as I. His unit was being transported by train to another part of the front at the time. I met him along the way, not far from Insterburg, and we travelled together in a cattle car for some time. As an officer I was able to get information about their destination, and also about when and where they would be stopping on their route. I gave my chauffeur instructions about the station to which he should come to pick me up again. This plan worked well and the two of us had important time together for sharing. I could not anticipate that later in life at our home church in Chilliwack, we would preach the message of peace from the same pulpit.

By Christmas the front was not very far from our home. The fighting subsided for a while, during which time I was granted a few days of home leave. Ernusch was five months pregnant by then. Thoughts about leaving their homes and heading west were on everybody's mind. However, the political climate was so totally controlled by the Nazi propaganda machine that few people had the courage to leave. Only Annchen, my brother Hans's wife with their children, and Gretel, my sister, left early enough to get to Hirschegg, Austria, where Annchen's sister lived.

I was taken back to the train station in a covered coach. That was the first leg of the trip back to the front line and to the battle. I had said good-bye to Gerd at Reichfelde. When we drove along the birch lane of our family's estate, I wept. I knew I would never see Reichfelde again. Ernusch accompanied me to Altfelde. The big question which hung between us was: "Will we ever see each other again?"

24. The Bitter End

Returning to the front, only a few hours from our home, brought the fate of the masses of refugees more clearly into mind. There were thousands, perhaps millions of them. Some travelled by horse and wagon; others on foot. All of them fled westward. My sister Magdalena, who lived close to Goldap with her husband Paul Schneiderreit and their family, moved to Reichfelde before Christmas. After returning to the front I was able to look into their home where everything had been left as if they were out for an evening visit and would be returning at any moment. It was a sad scene.

Our unit received an order from one of the senior generals to push all the refugees' vehicles off the road and into the ditches to give the army more room to manoeuvre. We always had to sign a paper when we received written orders. I personally signed that paper, then showed it to my Commander von Reuter and threw it into the fireplace in the house in which we had set up our "office."

Von Reuter was shocked. "What are you doing?" he demanded.

"Sir," I said, "I have signed for the receipt of that order, but nobody else under my command will ever see it." Under different circumstances, that action could have cost me my life.

On January 12, 1945, the Russian army's winter offensive began with heavy fire which descended on us like a volcano. The intense fighting continued for several weeks. By January 18 the Russian army broke through the German lines and took Tolkemit. They circled the area and cut off all the supplies for our units. Podzun wrote:

> Fighting for something which is already lost is a heavy burden on the mind of everyone. Hitler's oft-repeated command that every position was to be "defended to the last man" sounded very hollow to everyone. The men shook their heads when they heard it (Podzun, 27).

My friend Siegfried Ecker, who helped Ernusch when Bibi died, had returned to the front line, only to be wounded again. That was also the time when we had to dismiss Hans-Henning Podzun from the front line because he developed serious health problems.

On March 11 the Russian army's propaganda unit, using huge loudspeakers, offered us "heaven on earth." Pamphlets which rained down by the thousands from low-flying airplanes stated, "Comrades of the 21st Division, the war is hopelessly lost. Come over to us. Bring along your blankets and meal utensils" (Podzun, 27).

On March 22 the final Russian attack on the remaining German troops commenced. Because we had not seen a German airplane for a long time, the Russian planes could come in low with their bombs. I saw Major Wilhelm Beuttel, my close friend and neighbour from Reichfelde, jump into one of the many bomb craters when the attack began. That's where he died.

Next day we received an order that the remainder of the 21st Division should be pulled out of the area "to form a new fighting unit in Middle Germany." What a mockery! According to Podzun,

> On the beach called "Frisches Haff" between Rosenberg and Balga, there was absolute chaos. It was like Dunkirk. The wounded ones were lying on the beach by the hundreds, hopeless and without any protection. The heavy Russian artillery fire continued to rain down on them (Podzun, 32).

On March 27 what was left of the 21st Division was transported out of the area across the "Haff." Two days later the battle on the mainland of East Prussia was over.

My own Commander von Reuter died on the newly established front, west of Königsberg and close to Fischhausen. I was his Adjutant. As I write these memoirs, on the desk in front of me is a keepsake from him—a metal cup with his signature engraved on the bottom. He used it for coffee, beer, hard liquor and for brushing his teeth. I now use it for my paper clips.

In Pillau a new defence line was hastily established under the leadership of General Chill. The rest of Division 21 was gathered together in Regiment 45 under Major Jöres for whom I was adjutant. Pillau was lost the next day. From there we fought and then retreated from one position to the next toward Danzig. Podzun wrote the following about our departure:

When the front arrived in Kahlberg (the Baltic Sea resort about which we had such wonderful childhood memories), the order came to transport the rest of the Division to Kiel via Hela. Not everyone could be notified. The majority of the men in the 21st Infantry Division who received the order boarded the Hendrik Fisher V. in Hela (Podzun, 36).

In my dreams I sometimes still see the uncounted wounded or dead German soldiers lying on the shore of the "Frischen Haff" on April 18, 1945, the day a small group of our Regiment—me included—was picked up by that navy flagboat at night. Waves were breaking over the dead and wounded soldiers. Surely such a sight should have convinced me then that pacifism was the only sane response to killing and war.

On board the ship we had time to talk. "What do we do now?" we pondered. None of us knew anything about our families. Some had professions, such as Ohlerich who was an experienced lawyer, or Hans Kappis who was a forest ranger. I remarked that I planned to go into the ministry. With us also was Hans Höpfner, my "servant friend." For years he had cared for my horses, even when I was transferred to the Regiment's headquarters. He had also taken over responsibility for looking after my affairs when the man in charge had been killed by a grenade.

We landed in Kiel on May 1, the day Hitler committed suicide. The announcement came over the radio just as we were moving into our army barracks. No one expressed sadness or regret. Midst all the turmoil and chaos, we felt only relief.

A few days later, May 5, 1945, the war was over. Fifty-five million people had died, many millions were crippled for life. Rivers of tears were shed and pools of blood flowed. Millions in prisoner-of-war camps, especially those in Russia, suffered in indescribable ways. Podzun summed up the demise of Infantry 21 thus:

> After a short stay in Gettorf and Ellingstedt, a group from the 21st Infantry Division marched to Flensburg to "protect" the German Government office of Admiral Dönitz (the successor to Hitler as head of the German state). Before the last ones parted from each other a list was made of the names: Rev. Baumgartner, Captain Bohn, Sergeant Christof Zik, Major G. Collee, Captain Bartel. . . . Captain Kappis was there as well. The 21st Infantry Division was no more (Podzun, 36-37).

I had made many good friends—that's the only positive thing I could say about the war. When the war ended—and even more emphatically since—I echoed the words of General William T. Sherman, one of the great war heroes during the Civil War in the United States, "War is hell!"

III

Trying to Put Things Back Together Again

We left Germany for good. Germany: the land of our youth, with wonderful memories of home and family life on the farm; the land of our hopes and dreams; the land where I had joined the army in peacetime, not realizing what that would lead to; the land where we had left our firstborn behind on that little hill where his coffin was buried; the land where we struggled with new realities in the process of adjusting to the postwar era; the land that Ernusch and I were not sorry to leave behind. We were ready to begin anew.

25. New Beginnings

When our Division marched from Kiel toward Flensburg, we crossed the Kaiser Wilhelm Kanal, the channel which connected the Baltic Sea and the North Sea. At the time we did not know that we had entered the only territory in all of Germany which had been declared a "no war zone" by the Allied forces. Flensburg was the residence of Admiral Dönitz, the designated successor to Adolf Hitler, who had to sign the document for Germany to capitulate. Even the prisoner-of-war camps in that area seemed more like registration places than prisons.

The war was over. Everyone was looking for the best way of finding family members and going home—*if* they still had a home. Our deepest desire was to get back to normal life, if possible. Since I did not know if anyone from my family was still alive, I decided to look for a job within this "no war zone."

I still belonged to the 21st Division which was protecting the headquarters of Admiral Dönitz so I needed permission from the General to use an army vehicle with a driver. My friend Hans Kappis accompanied me to the agriculture office in Eckernförde. There I asked for the addresses of farms where all the sons had died during the war. The name I received was Frau Magnussen, Dörphof. The senior farmer had died shortly before the war. The oldest son had inherited the farm, but he and his two brothers died in action. The son was married but, since there were no children, Hitler's inheritance law (*Erbhofgesetz*) came into effect. That meant his only sister, not his wife, inherited the farm.

We drove to Dörphof immediately where I spoke to Mrs. Meier-Magnussen, the farm owner. Since she was inexperienced in farm management, her mother had taken full responsibility. Mrs. Magnussen was in the field so the daughter suggested that I go there to talk to her. I wonder what thoughts crossed Mrs. Magnussen's mind when she saw two army officers marching toward her out in the field. We met this gracious, heroic woman there on a farm pathway. Hans Kappis introduced himself as a forest ranger; I indicated I was a farmer and presented myself to her as a candidate to manage her farm. We walked to the farmhouse together where we had coffee with her, Mrs.

Meier-Magnussen and the son's widow who, according to the inheritance law, had no claim to the farm. Even though I did not possess a single document to prove my agricultural training, I got the job. We agreed that I would start as soon as possible and that I would bring Hans Höpfner along to be a farm worker.

The farmhouse was full of refugees who had come from the east and from the cities which had been destroyed by the bombings. Persons from six different families were housed in a building normally intended for the farmer's family. When I mentioned my family, it quickly became clear that, under the current circumstances, there would not be room for them in the farmhouse.

The reality was I did not even know if I had a family. Twelve million civilians had left the eastern part of Germany, fleeing west; 12 million people had fled from the Baltic Sea to the Austrian border. Approximately 10 million arrived in West Germany. Would Erna, nearly nine months pregnant, and 14-month-old Gerd be part of the 10 million or would they be among the two million who had perished?

Hans and I received special permission from prisoner-of-war officials to work at the farm. We had to continue wearing our uniforms because we did not yet have our release papers from the British army. On May 23, 1945, Hans Höpfner and I arrived in Dörphof. My Commander's chauffeur brought us to the farm in a military vehicle. I can still see that army car leaving the farm driveway on its way back to Flensburg. That was my last contact with the German Army which I had served for seven-and-a-half years.

Life on the farm resulted in a sudden and dramatic change in my daily routine. I knew nothing about my family's circumstances; I was not acquainted with farming practices in that area; I did not know anyone in the community besides the three women with whom I had coffee once. Suddenly I was responsible for running the farm.

Foreign workers were still being employed on farms in that area. At Dörphof, for example, the herdsman was a young Pole. He was extremely upset that, after a war in which Poland was one of the victors, he was now to have a young German officer as his boss. It posed such a serious problem for him that he quit the very first day. That provided an opportunity for Hans Höpfner, who had been a herdsman before he was drafted into the army, to take over that responsibility. What a comfort it was to have Hans around. But, as the teasing by the other farm workers indicated, he found it hard not to continue treating me as his "army superior."

The entrance to the farmhouse at Dörphof where I served as farm manager for six years after the war.

The abrupt change in my daily routine, the sudden removal of responsibilities affecting life and death, the long nights in comparison with the continuous go-go-go of the retreating German Army, and the weight of nagging doubts about my experience over the past years—what a heavy burden to live with. There were hours when I envied my many friends who had died.

For seven-and-a half years I and most others in that nation had convinced ourselves how important we were to the "Fatherland." An inner emptiness developed, darkened by the helplessness of not knowing anything about my family. Having slept only brief hours each night during the last several months, the nights became unbearably long. I started walking out on the fields in the evenings, sometimes for hours. Somehow the Lord had become distant and the "why" questions overwhelming.

Since the office of the 21st Division was still functioning in Flensburg, comrades heard of my whereabouts and came to visit me; for example, Siegfried Ecker, my close friend, who was in a hospital nearby. He had been heavily wounded and had to have part of his lung removed. Mrs. Magnussen was always gracious toward my friends, providing them with shelter and food.

26. Reunited with My Family

One day Hans-Henning Podzun arrived on the yard riding his army motorcycle. In the West he had become a British prisoner-of-war. When the fighting subsided he was installed by the British as military policeman in a German uniform but with a special sign on his arm. Now he was looking for opportunities to enter the work force. He wondered if he could begin an apprenticeship program on the farm. Because Hans-Henning had documents from the British Army----he was even allowed to fill up his motorcycle at their gasoline stations----I asked him to do me a big favour. Would he be willing to drive to Hoheneggelsen?

I knew that my sister, Ruth Schroeder, had been working as an organist in that village near Hannover since 1943. She was the only family member living in the British Zone. I wanted to know if Ruth knew anything about the rest of my family. From a postcard I had received during the chaotic time in East Prussia, all I knew was that my family had been on the westward trek with many others.

A few days later Hans-Henning made his way to Hoheneggelsen where he found not only my sister Ruth but also Ernusch and our two boys. They had heard in a round-about way that I might be in Schleswig-Holstein. My brother Walter had arrived in Hoheneggelsen earlier. While in a prisoner-of-war camp he had met a soldier who, when he heard Walter's family name, said, "I know a Captain Bartel who is in Schleswig-Holstein. I was in his unit. Here is my army passport which has his signature." Walter was sure that it was my writing but Ernusch was not fully convinced.

Hans-Henning gave Erna my message and Magnussen's invitation to come to Dörphof. On July 26 he returned to Dörphof and gave me detailed information from Ernusch about herself and other family members. He reported that the Mennonites of West Prussia had suffered severely along with millions of other German citizens who fled westward ahead of the advancing Russian army. Thousands had died on the road and on the Baltic Sea as the Russian bombs and torpedoes found them. The *Gustlow,* a large ocean liner, had been used for evacuating many refugees. It went down in the Baltic, taking with it many relatives of Ernusch's mother. Fortunately, Ernusch's mother, sister and sister-in-law with their families arrived safely in Denmark on another transport ship.

Ernusch had joined my parents and sisters on the westward trek from West Prussia. It had been an incredible journey. They travelled by horse and buggy during the cold winter months. She was eight months pregnant at the time and responsible for our 14-month-old son. They finally arrived in Hoheneggelsen during early April and Ernusch and Gerd had found refuge on the farm of the Westphal family. On April 11 Reinhard was born.

I had arrived in Kiel in May, one month after Ernusch reached her destination but, because of communication and transportation difficulties, it had taken another two months before we finally heard from each other. After several days in Dörphof with me, Hans-Henning headed back to Hoheneggelsen to help Ernusch and the boys make the move to Dörphof.

A complication developed before they left. One of the horses they had brought along from Reichfelde was my personal riding horse, Blütenfee. Would it be feasible to take her along to Dörphof? Toward the end of the long journey from the east she had not been able to pull her share of the load any more. My sisters, Hanna and Gertraut, knew how much I loved that horse and insisted on bringing her along. In a few months Blütenfee recovered her strength but she became difficult to handle. Part of my family was concerned that Hans-Henning would not be able to manage her, and were worried about the safety of Erna and the boys on the journey. The confusion was finally ironed out, and a few days later they were on the road.

The covered wagon carried a mattress, Hans-Henning's 500 cc BMW motorcycle, feed for the horses, food for the travellers and those belongings which Ernusch had packed up for the trek from Reichfelde. Reinhard was placed in a baby carriage behind the driver's seat occupied by Hans-Henning. Gerd sat in a special spot beside him.

That "odd couple" and the two young boys were on the road for approximately eight days. They found shelter for the night mostly in rural homes along the way. When Ernusch and the boys were invited to stay in the house for night, Hans-Henning used the mattress in the wagon; when that was not possible, Ernusch and Gerd utilized the mattress and Hans-Henning found shelter in the hay barn. The people they met fully understood their travel arrangements. Millions of Germans were on the road trying to find their families.

As they neared Dörphof Ernusch mentioned to Hans-Henning that, in spite of her excitement about being reunited with me, she had some uneasy feelings about what was going to happen. How right she was. The day before they arrived I received a stern order from the British occupation forces to report to one of their camps immediately to process my release from the army. I had no option but to go. Erna's disappointment at not finding me in Dorphöf was understandable.

Two days after Ernusch, the boys and Hans-Henning arrived, I returned. Finally, we were all together again. We were among the fortunate ones. The Mennonites who remained in West Prussia and those who were captured by the advancing Russian army suffered horrendous persecution. Poland wanted nothing to do with Germans.

In his story of the Mennonites in Poland and Prussia, Peter J. Klassen reports that Cornelius Dirksen, elder of the Thiensdorf congregation, declined to flee to the west. Consequently, in 1947 he was expelled from the new Poland. "With this," writes Klassen, "the story of Mennonites in West Prussia came to an end" (Klassen, *A Homeland for Strangers*, 88).

27. Post-War Struggles

The realities of my new life took a while to sink in: I was reunited with my family, and the war was behind us. We were together again, united for the rest of our lives after so many years of tearful partings, joyful embraces during brief reunions, many letters, and countless prayers for each other during the long, lonely nights. There would be no more saying good-bye to Erna and the boys.

For many years, as a professional and as an officer, war had been my vocation. How else could I justify my actions? As a Christian, a child of God, how could I have survived spiritually? Now all that thinking lay in shambles. The *umsonst* feeling—the doubts that what I had been doing was all for naught; that it had been done in vain, for no reason; that it had no value whatsoever—was a heavy burden on my mind.

Then there was Ernusch. She and I had shared our innermost feelings and aspirations in hundreds, perhaps thousands of letters, during the war. But now that there was peace, life was so different than we had dreamed it would be. We were in Dörphof and reunited but we were not at home.

Our family's accommodation was one small room. It had barely enough space for beds for the four of us. To get to our room we had to go through another bedroom where a father and his two adult daughters lived. It was a typical arrangement at that time, with several households sharing a house which was meant for one family.

But that was not the hardest part. During the three months prior to Ernusch's coming, my free time had been spent with the three Magnussen women. In some ways I had become part of the family and the farming operation. That changed when Hans Meier, husband of Mrs. Meier-Magnussen, the farm owner, was released from the prisoner-of-war camp. He had been an officer in the Marine Maintenance Corps. Mr. Meier was a likeable fellow, but he had one major problem. He was dishonest and apparently believed his own lies. On his return he joined our little farm community and began an apprenticeship position with me. A man trained for office work in maintaining the war machinery of the Marines, he suddenly found himself on a farm, needing to work physically and to adjust to farm and family life in strange ways. Besides that, he had to take advice from everybody.

At first Hans Meier's arrival on the scene was a great relief for the three Magnussen women. Now there was a man in this circle of very diverse women. Mrs. Magnussen, Sr., heroic and honourable, was a strong person, clear in her decision-making but always reserved. She was the only church-goer in the family but, like almost everyone else, was a heavy cigarette smoker. And she was devoted to her two little Dackels. Mrs. Meier-Magnussen, the owner of Dörphof, was pregnant with her first child. She did not know how to deal with her farming responsibilities. Her marriage partner was a man whom she admired as a beautiful dancing partner, but whom she learned to dislike, even despise, because he was so dishonest. Finally, there was Mrs. Magnussen, Jr., widow of the son who originally inherited the farm. She had no right to the farm after her husband was killed in the war although a child would have been eligible for inheritance. She liked to ride horses, including my Blütenfee.

Since our family lived in such a small room, we were invited to eat with the Magnussen family. Gerd was not yet two years old then. To have him at a formal meal table sometimes caused our emotions to go up and down like a roller coaster.

For many years both Ernusch and I had lived quite independently, except during holiday time. Now the demands of my job, the obligation to relate to the Magnussens, the need to adjust to peacetime, and the emotional and spiritual turmoil which my war experiences were causing within me were hard on both of us. More than once Ernusch wished that we could leave Dörphof. But that point in history, when millions of Germans didn't have enough to feed their children while we had plenty for ourselves and were even able to help others, was not the time to consider leaving.

Our living conditions at Dörphof improved significantly when we were able to move into a different part of the house, an apartment vacated by a woman with two daughters who moved back to her home city of Kiel. There Ernusch had her own kitchen and we were able to separate our personal affairs from the Magnussen family. In the meantime, Hans Höpfner had found his family. They were assigned to a suite in the farm labourers' apartment block. Their eldest daughter, Elly, who was old enough to be looking for a job, assisted Ernusch with the children and with the housework.

In summer 1948 Christoph was born. Then we received use of an additional small room adjacent to our apartment which had been the senior Mrs. Magnussen's private room. Other improvements were made. During the first years all the families living in the farmhouse had to use a hand pump in the annex of the farmhouse for their water; the only available toilets were outhouses. In 1946-47, when black market activity reached its zenith, we were able to get the living quarters of the farm owner's house supplied with running water and a bathroom, all in exchange for one pig. We still did not have access to indoor plumbing.

About the time when Christoph was born Mrs. Meier-Magnussen gave birth to her second daughter. Soon thereafter the Meier-Magnussen marriage started to deteriorate and the relationship between the two became unbearable. Mr. Meier and Mrs. Meier-Magnussen would take turns coming to speak to me about the situation. Her dislike of him increased so much that separation was unavoidable. Divorce followed. He went to university to study agriculture and later became a well-accepted teacher.

Mrs. Meier-Magnussen, free now, started flirting with Mr. Schulz-Pilgram, a new man I had employed on the farm. This fine, energetic person had been wounded during the war, resulting in an obvious limp. One day he told me that within a few days he would inform me how long I would be keeping my job. He already saw himself as the next farm manager. It did not turn out as Mr. Schulz-Pilgram had hoped. Mrs. Meier-Magnussen moved on to a different relationship with Dr. Francke, a surgeon from the neighbouring town of Kappeln who had divorced his wife earlier. They were married in spring 1950. After Dr. Francke moved into Dörphof it became evident to us rather quickly that our time there would soon be over.

The Magnussen-Bartel relationship went through all kinds of tests. One Sunday afternoon we planned to take a buggy ride through the fields to the shore of the Baltic Sea. I had bought a horse to match Blütenfee and hitched them to a coach which had room for six people. I took my position in the driver's box and Ernusch sat beside me. The Magnussen women were seated inside the coach. Mr. Meier was the last one out of the house and became visibly upset when he noticed what the seating arrangement was to be. Apparently he had planned to sit beside me.

In a chiding tone he asked Erna, "And where should I sit?"

Erna was somewhat baffled by his attitude and blurted out, "Perhaps you can run behind the coach." Understandably, that was not a helpful retort. He turned around and walked back into the house. His wife, who had been sitting in the coach already followed him. The two other women did the same. I uncoupled the horses, hitched Blütenfee to my one-horse carriage and Ernusch and I left for a drive by ourselves.

Other differences of opinion arose. We were happy when Ernusch was expecting Christoph and did not detect any negative reaction from the Magnussen family. The day after Chris was born the accountant from Kiel, a Mr. Bückert, was there to work on the books. In the morning I cheerfully entered the Magnussen living room where he was working and announced the arrival of a baby boy.

Bückert said reproachfully, "Do you really think that as a farm manager you should have an additional child?"

I was surprised and, looking him straight in the eye, said, "Do you think I will remain a farm manager all my life?" I left the room, deeply hurt. I never discovered the extent to which his comment represented the thinking of the Magnussen family.

In spring 1950, our son Siegfried Alexander (Alex) was born. Now we had four boys. After Elly Höpfner found a different job in Dörphof, where a new clothing factory had been established, her younger sister Anni came to assist Ernusch with the household chores and with child-care. She was a great help. Christoph became especially attached to her. By then Gerd had started school and took his responsibility as the eldest very seriously. We could depend on him totally. One day, when he was six, Ernusch sent him to the grocery store about a kilometre away to buy something. Four-year-old Reinhard accompanied him. On the way home Reinhard saw Elly Höpfner through one of the windows in the factory where she was working. He decided to stay with her and, try as they might, Elly and Gerd could not persuade him to return home. Elly had to phone us to get help for poor Gerd.

I recall another incident which involved Reinhard. Close to the back entrance of the house was a small, rather deep pool, a build-up of drainage water from the manure pile. During the winter months it was frozen solid and the children spent hours playing on it. One evening Ernusch and I came home from visiting and found that Anni had put Reinhard to bed early. Apparently, the children had been playing at the pool, not knowing that someone had cut a hole in the ice. Reinhard had fallen in, wearing heavy winter clothing. His hair was wet so obviously he had gone in all the way, but he had been able to pull himself out, nobody knew how. Anni had given him a bath and put him to bed by the time we returned home. We thanked the Lord from the bottom of our hearts that we found him alive and well.

The relationship of our children to the other children on the farm was always a joy to see. Also, the Magnussen family was very tolerant toward all of them. Once when the children were quite noisy in front of the senior Mrs. Magnussen's living room, she opened the window to shush them up. She had forgotten that the outside double window had no hinges. All the children, except Reinhard, quickly disappeared. The window fell out and landed squarely on our three-year-old son. Standing there, fenced-in by the window frame, shattered glass strewn all around him, little Reinhard was perplexed. He did not know what had hit him.

28. Farming in Dörphof

The Magnussen estate had about the same acreage as our home farm in Reichfelde, approximately 125 hectares. The information I had received at the agriculture office about Dörphof was: "Small herd of cattle and a high amount of debt." After I had been there only two years, Mrs. Meier-Magnussen decided that we should join a modern agricultural counselling agency based in Kappeln which would analyze all parts of the farming operation. Perhaps the best way of describing my work at Dörphof is to quote from a report by Mr. Bernhard Wermke, director of the agency. On September 19, 1950, he evaluated my work thus:

> . . . Mr. Siegfried Bartel is a refugee, married with four children. He has been the sole manager of Dörphof since 1945. Because of circumstances during the war, Dörphof was not in the best condition. In a very short time, Mr. Bartel was able to bring Dörphof into high production. Today it is one of the top producers in the farming area of Eckernförde. Through industrious reorganization Mr. Bartel established a foundation which would allow Dörphof to survive even in a time of crisis. His agricultural accomplishments are far above average and have reached a level that would be hard to surpass.

The increase in cultivation of sugar beets and cattle beets from nine percent to 34 percent was an achievement arrived at in only three years. The cattle operation was brought from average to a high level of production in a very short time. There has been a substantial increase in the number of cows. The hog farming operation was completely reorganized and improved, resulting in a high percentage of profit. The buildings were brought up to standard, especially the apartments for the farm worker families which were renovated and improved. The drainage system for Dörphof was improved by establishing a new system and extending the old one.

All in all, through his action Dörphof has achieved stability for the future. The improvements mentioned before were only possible through Mr. Bartel's personal activity and his ability to combine theory and practice in an above average way.

Reliability, absolute honesty and a healthy ambition to be successful are his outstanding characteristics. The farm workers have high respect for him both as a friend and as their superior. These two combined give him authority.

I personally found Mr. Bartel a sincere man and a passionate farmer. I hope that some time in the future he will be able to farm his own soil.

What I had experienced with farm management in Prussia was also customary in that part of Germany: the manager did no manual labour. He arranged and divided up daily tasks among the workers, then observed and supervised the operation.

I used my own riding horse, Blütenfee, to get around the farm. Often I would take advantage of the opportunity to ride through the woods and along the shore of the Baltic Sea. I know that some people criticized me for that. Yet, everybody knew that Blütenfee was my own horse and many understood that a former officer in the army would find riding a helpful way to adjust back to normal life after the war.

And for me riding, certainly was a hobby. After the war I organized the first hunt in the area for our riding club. In fall we enjoyed similar hunts sponsored by different hosts. In summer 1949 I was in charge when our club planned and managed a riding competition in Kappeln with over 100 riders and horses competing. It was a complete success.

I had an excellent relationship with all the farm workers and enjoyed their company. The wages, paid in the almost worthless *Reichsmark*, gave very little incentive for working hard. The main support for families were the provisions in kind so all people working on the farm at least had enough to eat. They had their own chickens, ducks, geese and could feed a few pigs.

29. First Experiences in Public Life

Like uncontrolled waves of the sea, millions of refugees had streamed from eastern to western Germany. Many had settled in Schleswig-Holstein. In numerous villages and towns the proportion of local inhabitants to refugees was one to three. That situation became even more drastic in areas where army barracks, some unused, became holding camps for refugees. Tensions between the two groups were unavoidable and at times reached dangerous levels.

A new organization was set up to protect the interests of the refugees. The Association of People Banished from Their Homeland (*Bund der Heimat Vertriebenen*) became the refugees' mouthpiece. After checking it out, I became involved in the organization. In a few years I accepted the position of president in the county (*Kreis*) of Eckernförde, an area with over 10,000 refugees. As always in organizations like that, the radical element was the most outspoken; consequently the more moderate ones had a hard time with leaders.

During my time as president I began my training in public speaking, invaluable experience for my involvements later in Canada. Sometimes I gave presentations at refugee rallies two or three times a week. Public transportation had become a problem, so I rode on Blütenfee or took the buggy, occasionally even went by bicycle.

Working for that refugee organization had its own special challenges. Because of my employment with a local, well established farm family, I was automatically placed on the side of the wealthy, of those who had not lost money or property. Yet I was really one of the have-nots—the only material possession I had was my trusted horse which was rescued from the past. Hence I was in the predicament of belonging to both sides, a situation which proved both an advantage and a disadvantage. I was severely tested when, at public meetings and rallies, I took a strong position against radicals in the refugee movement and promoted a conciliatory course between the parties involved. Settling differences in such a setting was not only a meaningful beginning to involvement in public life but also another step on the road to embracing a pacifist lifestyle.

After the war ended, the first election for local council was announced. I decided to run for a seat as alderman. In their election system there was no candidate for mayor, but the alderman with the highest number of votes would automatically take that position. The results showed that I had won. Second highest was the previous mayor, a highly respected farmer with deep understanding for the destiny of the refugees.

I had decided for myself that a native of Schleswig-Holstein should be mayor. At the first meeting of council, I stunned the people present by announcing that I did not accept the traditional procedure and nominated my runner-up to be mayor. It was proven over and over again that that was the best decision with respect to my effectiveness on council as representative of the refugees. I became the deputy mayor, thereby the second member on the regional district council.

All meetings were held in a private room at the *Gasthaus*. By North American standards, the German *Gasthaus* was like a small motel with a few rooms for night lodging, a coffee shop which served hot meals, and the local pub. Those meetings in the *Gasthaus*, some charged with heated arguments, were often accompanied and influenced by the availability of alcohol. In wintertime it was *grog* (hot water, sugar and a varying amount of rum); in summer the standard beverage was beer. The overall working relationship and atmosphere were very good. The responsibility of representing the refugees on that municipal council gave me a great deal of satisfaction.

My experience with the refugee committee and my role in municipal politics must have been the reason that, in fall of 1950, I was approached by representatives of the Christian Democratic Union (CDU) to let my name stand as candidate for a member of parliament in the "Land Schleswig Holstein" (equivalent to the Canadian provincial legislature). The election was scheduled for spring 1951.

30. Decision to Leave

In spite of the fact that we had enough to eat and that I had a secure place of employment, we knew we could not live forever with the tensions which accompany living in a state of "dependency." Living under one roof with so many people was sometimes extremely difficult, especially for Ernusch.

Our most difficult period in Dörphof began one night in fall of 1950 when the farmhouse where we all lived burned down. Günter Remien, one of the neighbours, came home on his motorcycle in the early morning hours from a visit with his fiancée in Kappeln. From some kilometres away he saw a glare in the sky. As he got closer, he realized that the thatch roof of the farmhouse was ablaze. As he drove into the farmyard he blew his horn to awaken all of us who were asleep in the house. We had only minutes to escape the inferno. The doorway to our apartment was at the gable end, so we had a little more time to get out than those who lived close to the main entrance. Most of our belongings were saved, except the winter clothing which we had stored in the attic.

Once I got out of the burning building, I ran to the granary at the end of the barn where the main panel which controlled the electricity supply for the whole farm was located. I quickly disconnected the power going to the burning house. There I found a fairly thick wire which had been used to "repair" the main fuse for the house. At that time it was almost impossible to buy replacement fuses and the seven families in the house, many of them using hot plates for cooking, always overextended the normal use of power. I did not know who had used that method of replacing the fuse, but I immediately put the piece of wire into my pocket. We were successful in saving the barn in spite of the fact that the house and barn were only about six metres apart and that the roof of the barn was covered with tar paper.

There were many refugees from eastern Germany in the area. The fact that I was leader of the refugee assistance organization may have contributed to the fact that so much from our apartment was carried out of the burning house. Another reason simply was that the main entrance to the house was engulfed in flames before the door to our apartment was. That night our children were given over to the care of the Höpfner family and we found shelter with the Dibberns, our farm neighbours. Eventually we were able to get one large room with an extra entrance and a hallway that could be used as a kitchen. That's where we as a family lived for the rest of our time in Dörphof. I arranged a small garret at the Magnussen farm as my office.

Naturally the insurance company had special interest in finding the cause of the fire, so a police investigation began immediately. A team of investigators, including a woman interrogator, arrived and started their interviews. A young man who worked at the farm and lived in an upstairs apartment mentioned that Ernusch and Anni Höpfner had been in the attic two days before the fire, using a candle for light because there was no electricity in that part of the house. The third-floor attic was used to store loose grain in large piles and to leave luggage for which we did not have room in our apartments.

The theory which the police invented was that Ernusch had left her candle in the attic and it set fire to the grain. They interviewed several people to try and confirm their position. The last person they questioned was Anni, who had been in the attic with Ernusch. When they asked Anni to confirm that the candle had been left upstairs she vehemently denied it.

The interviewer persisted until Anni screamed, "It's not true! It's not true!" and suffered a nervous breakdown. The police took no heed and charged Ernusch with arson through neglect. I was never interviewed, but had that piece of wire as evidence in my pocket.

We hired the best lawyer to defend Ernusch. When the day of the court case arrived, we went to Eckernförde. The public prosecutor presented the case in an inflammatory and prejudiced way, which frightened us very much.

Every time the judge turned to our lawyer and asked, "Have you something to say?" he replied, "No comment." But when he began his defence, he shredded the prosecutor's presentation to pieces. The judge's verdict: "Not guilty."

That acquittal had a number of consequences. First, the burden of being unfairly accused was removed. Secondly, all the other parties living in the house had received fire insurance money, but we had not. Immediately after the court decision we received ours as did the Magnussen family. Thus they were able to build a new house. That was the most crucial question for them and for us. If the reason for the fire had been traced to the "jumped" fuse, then the payment of the fire insurance money to the Magnussen family would have been in question. Lastly, a guilty verdict would definitely have brought us to a higher court. Such a delay might have affected our plans for the future.

After that ordeal Ernusch desperately needed some time for emotional healing and relaxation in a different environment. The parents of our friend Christoph Nehring offered her that kind of "oasis" to recover in Düsseldorf. It was there that she collapsed, but the Nehring friendship helped her to recover.

When she returned to Dörphof, our relationship to the Francke-Magnussen family was more reserved than it had been. Dr. Francke tried to become more involved in the management of the farm. I had been very generous in paying wages to the workers. Dr. Francke imposed limitations which I could not accept. He also asked me to compromise my principles in other aspects of relating to the people with whom I worked.

In December 1950 I informed them that I would not renew my contract after its expiry date on March 31, 1951. To give up a secure position appeared to be an irresponsible decision, considering the family's well-being. By making that decision, I also disqualified myself from being a candidate for a member of parliament in the area.

But as those doors closed, others were opening.

31. Where to Now?

For more than 400 years our Mennonite forebears had farmed the land in the Vistula-Nogat Delta in West Prussia. During that time they had developed and nurtured their church life. They held to their unique interpretation of the gospel of Jesus Christ. However, most people in my parents' generation had changed their attitude with regard to service in the army—and my generation had completed that process by going off to war.

Mennonites did retain their traditional emphasis on a strong belief and value system. Yet, as so often happens with tradition, the ideal is very different than the reality. That also applied to the principle of "baptism on confession of faith." For the majority in our congregations that belief had deteriorated to a formality. But for most in our families, and in a special way for Ernusch and me, baptism was an act of obedience based on deep conviction.

Many ethnic Mennonites in West Prussia did not attend church at all. Also, a large number of church members did not participate actively in church life. In Germany it had been the custom for Lutherans, Catholics and Mennonites alike to belong to a church only so they had a place to be married and buried.

A minority in the Mennonite churches of West Prussia did take the relationship to Jesus very seriously. Those nurtured by the Pietist movement, the evangelical *Gemeinschaftsbewegung* (revival movement), and those believers for whom the confession of faith was foundational formed the backbone of the Mennonite church.

Woher? From where had we come? What remained of the basics of Anabaptist principles? Ernusch and I remained fully dedicated to Jesus Christ as Lord and Saviour, but at that time the peace position was a non-issue. We strongly held to the position that child baptism was wrong. Instead we dedicated our sons to our Lord.

On the question *Wohin?*—Where shall we go?—our partial answer came when we established a relationship with the local Lutheran church, where we attended on Sunday mornings and sang in the church choir. Occasionally we went to a Mennonite service in Kiel, 70 kilometres away. We could go there only after I had bought a motorcycle—and then without children. Through that group we kept in touch with other Mennonites and because of that contact we were included in relief distribution from Mennonites in North America through Mennonite Central Committee (MCC). How thankful we were for the "towel parcels" (*Handtuch Päckchen*) which our children received. Each parcel, which included one outfit of clothing and a New Testament, was rolled into a large towel.

It was through the Kiel church connection that MCC received information of our whereabouts. In late fall 1945, C.F. Klassen, the MCC representative in Europe, knocked on our door in Dörphof for the first time. That great man of God was searching all over western Europe for the "lost Mennos." I was deeply impressed that a man from America—who of us in Germany really knew the difference between a U.S. and a Canadian person?—came to look us up. Only a few months earlier Americans had been "our enemies."

The first time C.F. Klassen came to see us, we still did not know the whereabouts of Ernusch's parents. We were in contact with her only brother, Alfred, but had no information about the rest of the family. We had reason to hope that they were all in Denmark. When C.F. Klassen showed us the list of Mennonites in Denmark, we found the names Emil and Clara Siebert, but behind Clara Siebert's name was a cross (+). In German files that sign usually indicated "deceased." What a shock for my Ernusch. We hoped that the sign might have a different meaning.

However, later it was confirmed that Mother Siebert, the wonderful woman she was, had died of a contagious disease just when the war ended. Occasionally she had mentioned her longing to be with the Lord, and my Ernusch had always responded, "Mutti, you cannot go now. Your praying power is so crucial until I am reunited with Siegfried." Mutti Siebert had been laid to rest in the *Helden Friedhof*, a well kept cemetery in Oksböl, where thousands of refugees and soldiers were buried.

Woher? Wohin? The challenge for us was to find answers to those questions for the future. A large group of Mennonites from West Prussia who were also in search of new beginnings had emigrated to Uruguay. Among them were many of Ernusch's cousins and their families and two of our neighbours from Reichfelde. At one time I even bought a German-Spanish dictionary, but Ernusch did not want to go to a country with a hot climate.

Meanwhile, my brother Hans and his family with my parents and siblings Gertraut, Hanna, Walter and Gretel, had found refuge in Viesenhaüserhof near Stuttgart in southern Germany. My sister Gertraut's brother-in-law Otto Hörr had connections with the local government and was able to help the Bartel family settle there.

Ernusch's father, her brother Alfred with family, and the Ernst Quapp and Hermann Pauls families——their wives were Ernusch's sisters——also found refuge there. Alfred Siebert and Ernst Quapp found jobs in the Viesenhaüserhof operation. In 1949-50 the government decided to rent out small parcels of land to individuals. My brother Hans managed two plots, one for his family and one for my parents. He could have made his living there, but he and brother Walter decided to pursue the option of emigrating to Canada.

They were in fairly close contact with C.F. Klassen. He also knew our family friend, David Rempel in British Columbia, Canada, whose passage to Canada had been financed by my parents and Ernusch's uncle in 1927. When Rempel heard that our family had lost everything, he had said to C.F. Klassen, "Find me the Heinrich Bartel family. I will help them all start a new life in Canada." After contacting "Onkel" Rempel, Hans and his family and Walter decided to take the big step and emigrate. Ernusch and I with our four boys up in northern Germany had no idea what the rest of our family was planning.

In summer 1950 MCC and the South German Mennonites had established a second Old Folks' Home which was located in Enkenbach. Herbert, son of C.F. Klassen, and his wife Maureen write in their book on CF's life:

> The second home for the elderly, *Friedensort* (Peaceful Refuge) was opened in October 1950 and CF had the joy of attending its dedication in Enkenbach near Kaiserslautern. . . . The home could accommodate 75 residents, and the house parents were his friends Heinrich and Hanna Bartel, whom he first got to know in Danzig back in 1930 at the second World Conference. . . .
>
> Just before Christmas, on December 17th, CF was back in Enkenbach at the Old Peoples' Home to join in the celebration of the Bartel's Silver Wedding. CF really enjoyed this kind of family celebration and was delighted to be there. The Bartels were greatly appreciated as house parents and for this special celebration their children had arrived as well—all, that is, but Walter their youngest,

who had left for Canada a few weeks previously (Herbert and Maureen Klassen, *Ambassador to His People*, 207-208).

I travelled to Enkenbach for the anniversary celebration without Ernusch and the boys. Our Alexander was only seven months old and it was winter. When I arrived I was shocked to hear all the news. More than that, I was upset that no one had notified us in Schleswig-Holstein about the opportunities and the offer from Onkel Rempel.

Walter had already left for Canada; Hans and family were scheduled to leave in April 1951. Onkel Rempel had sponsored both of them and was in the process of finding and purchasing a farm for Hans. Now another sponsorship was necessary. C.F. Klassen promised me that he would do everything he could to get us as a family into the same transport to Canada with Hans, Annchen and family.

I went home to Dörphof with the news for Ernusch! The *wohin*—where to go—had been answered. The rest was in C.F. Klassen's and the Lord's hands.

32. Destination Canada

On my return from Enkenbach, a few days before Christmas 1950, all thoughts focused on: *Destination*: Canada—and Ernusch did not know anything till I arrived home in Dörphof. There still were a few obstacles that could have influenced our new plan of going to Canada. Would Onkel C.F. Klassen have a sponsor on hand in such a short time so that we would be able to travel together with Hans and Annchen in April 1951? Would Onkel Rempel *really* be willing to help also us start farming? Would we pass the medical examination as a family? (Reinhard had a touch of tuberculosis as a two-year-old. Would that show on his x-ray?) The most crucial question: Would I, with my past as an officer in the German Army, be accepted by Canadian Immigration?

Although the Mennonite refugees who were born in Russia had received German citizenship, they were classified by the Commissioner of Refugees of the United Nations as displaced persons (DPs). MCC had been extremely busy with that group from 1945 to 1948. Toward the end of 1949 the majority of them had been processed and Canada began to accept "German-born" immigrants. That was the time we applied. My brother Walter was in the very first transport on the ship *Beaverbrae* where people from that group were included.

Despite great obstacles C.F. Klassen and his MCC team had already helped many but, as Herbert and Maureen Klassen wrote:

CF received a great shock when on July 23, 1949, IRO-Geneva (International Refugee Organization) issued an order that virtually stopped all Mennonite movements from Europe to both the US and Canada. He immediately went to Geneva and found out that the IRO eligibility officer reported that 3 to 40 percent of all Mennonite refugees had served in the German armed forces and had taken up German citizenship voluntarily, not under duress, as was at first believed. CF challenged these facts and figures, but at this stage the Order stood firm:

1. No Mennonite who had become a German citizen was entitled to IRO help.

2. The processing of all Mennonites was to be halted immediately (with the exception of those who had already obtained a Canadian visa).

3. All Mennonites, who had already passed the IRO-eligibility test, be processed again with special attention to their German naturalization and military service. . . .

After nine weeks of praying and working and waiting, the breakthrough came. He wrote, *Today, September 26th, I received the happy news by telephone from Geneva, that the obstructive clause has been removed and that a new draft is being prepared. I am to come to Geneva as soon as possible. The Lord has done it. His hour came, and with it the answer to many prayers* (Klassen, 195-196).

My concern for acceptance as an immigrant to Canada was not unfounded. In addition, my status as a former officer (captain) might be held against me. Nevertheless, on my arrival back in Dörphof after I had begun the emigration procedure in Enkenbach, things began to fall into place.

My contract with Mrs. Francke-Magnussen was running out on March 31, 1951. I had informed her that I would not continue working for her after that date. Shortly after Christmas we received confirmation from C.F. Klassen that Peter and Cornelius Kröker from Manitoba, half-brothers of Jakob Kröker, Wernigerode, were willing to sponsor us (Jakob Kröker was my brother Hans's father-in-law). Hans and his family were supported by Onkel David Rempel of Sumas, B.C. We soon received word from Onkel Rempel that he indeed was willing to help us get established in Canada. The first two concerns were taken care of. Apprehensively we wondered: "How would Canadian immigration officials respond to the other two?"

During that time of waiting we tried to carry on without too much disruption. From January to March we were preoccupied with planning, but always kept asking the big question: Will we be successful in getting the emigration visa? In the middle of March we received news that our turn to appear before the Canadian immigration officials had been set for the first days in April. I made arrangements to rent a car----which was already possible at that time. At noon on March 31 we received the telephone call to come immediately to the immigration office in Karlsruhe. That was my last day of work in Dörphof. An hour after work that evening we left for Karlsruhe.

Karlsruhe was in the section of Germany which was occupied by the United States Army. Many homes of the well-to-do had been taken over. The Canadian immigration office was in one such private villa. First we were sent to another building for our health examinations. Fearfully we approached that process. What a feeling of elation when we heard the words, "Everyone's O.K!" The third hurdle had been overcome. Then came what, in my estimation, was the most crucial phase of our application process. Would my participation as an officer in the German Army be the factor that would shatter our hopes of emigrating?

The dining room of that villa, with all its original furniture intact, was the waiting room. While we sat there, waiting for the crucial interview, C.F. Klassen walked in, talked with us for a while and handed out chocolates to the children. Then he briefly stepped into the office. When he left, he wished us all the best.

When my name was called----Ernusch and the boys were not included in the interview----I was extremely nervous. How surprised I was when the interviewing officer, who spoke fluent German, asked me only a few general questions. I was sitting across the table from him. On the application form I could see, written in large letters across the document, K L A S S E N. That explained the reason for the short, very formal interview. No questions about my past, despite the fact that I had been an officer in the German Army. Even though I had no regrets about my participation in the war, I was extremely happy that I was spared any dialogue about my past.

With our stamp and signature on the passport we received our immigration visa for Canada. We were informed that we would sail on April 28 on the *Beaverbrae*. The decision was made; all the obstacles were removed. We had only about three weeks to get ready to leave. From Karlsruhe we travelled to Viesenhäuserhof to consult with Hans and Annchen with whom we would be travelling. Then we went to say farewell to Ernusch's father and family members. For Ernusch the good-bye to Vater Siebert was the hardest part of leaving. He loved his youngest daughter dearly and was very sad because he knew he would not see her again. We made two more stopovers on the way back to Dörphof: Enkenbach where my parents lived, and Düsseldorf to see our friend Christoph Nehring and his parents.

After we arrived back in Dörphof, activity moved into high gear. We had only two weeks to get ready for the voyage to another continent. The boys went with Anni to the Höpfner family; Ernusch and I moved to the Gasthaus Remien to make it easier to dissolve our household in a hurry. But what was I to do with Blütenfee, my wonderful riding horse? Mrs. Magnussen, Jr., now married to a friend of Magnussen's second oldest son, was willing to take the horse. The act of separating myself from Blütenfee was filled with a great deal of symbolic meaning. Only someone who has spent many hours, even days over a period of years, in the saddle could understand what that parting meant. It symbolized the final separation from a lifestyle of the past.

The riding horse was also a symbol of my growing-up years in Reichfelde. It had been the status symbol of the young farm manager in Reichfelde, the *Junger Herr* (young master), who did no manual work but rode from field to field and observed the activities of the workers. The horse had been my steady companion. Furthermore, during my first years in the army, horses had been part of the relaxation and enjoyment. At Dörphof Blütenfee contributed to my reconciliation with the past. That black beauty was more sensitive than any horse I had ever ridden. I spent many hours on her, riding through fields and woods, adjusting to the cold reality of the present while clinging to the lifestyle of the past—all that was coming to an abrupt end.

Blütenfee had always been very nervous when she saw a train. Now I had to take her to the station and put her into a cattle car to have her transported to Westfalia. This time she walked into the cattle wagon without protesting. This time the locomotive did not bother her. Perhaps she sensed the sadness of the hour for both of us. When the train left the station, that chapter of the past was closed——forever.

During our final two weeks of getting ready we experienced the value of friendship in a special way. Some people built chests for packing our belongings. Edith Voll, Ernusch's friend, sewed coats and other clothing for the boys. Tante Abt, an aunt of our friend Hans Höpfner, knit shawls, gloves and toques for the boys. Ernusch

With Erna and the boys (from left), Alex, Reinhard, Christoph and Gerd, ready to leave for Canada in April 1951.

and I did the shopping and organizing. The final packing was done under supervision of the customs officers.

Hans Höpfner accompanied us on the local train to the station at Eckernförde where we boarded another train for the port of Bremerhafen. It was especially symbolic that our final farewell from Dörphof was the separation from Hans. He had been a long-time comrade during the war and a companion during the time of adjustment to normal life in peace time.

In preparation for our entry into Canada we all had to get various vaccinations. When we arrived in Bremerhafen we realized that Alex, not quite 12 months old, had developed a high temperature. We decided not to call the doctor at that time—we had some medication with us—because we were afraid we might not be allowed to board the *Beaverbrae* with a sick child.

Our friend Thea came by bicycle to see us off. And then there was C.F. Klassen who was present to oversee our boarding on the *Beaverbrae*.

In the waiting room he turned to Hans and me and said: "Boys, when you get to Canada and see the farming there, you will think they are doing everything wrong (we both had a college diploma in agriculture). Be silent for five years before you speak up. And one more thing: Continue to nourish the sense of family life."

When we boarded the *Beaverbrae* the person in charge of loading insisted that the playpen which Erna had brought for Alex should be stored in the luggage compartment. She refused to let them take it. It was so good that she had been adamant and had not given up the playpen. There was just enough room for it in the middle of the cabin for the night. In the daytime it was put on Ernusch's bunk so Alex had his private area there.

I was in a room with eight men; Hans and Annchen had a private room for their large family. Those arrangements were possible because of C.F. Klassen's connections and care. There were only five or six rooms of that size available. The rest of the approximately 2,000 passengers were in huge rooms on that vessel which had been used to transport troops across the Atlantic.

Toward evening the *Beaverbrae* lifted anchor. Our parting thoughts were, "*Destination*: Canada."

33. Voyage across the Ocean

As we saw the German coastline disappearing, we gathered with the boys in the cabin where Ernusch was staying and united in prayer, asking the Lord for guidance and protection. Alex's health was heavy on our mind. The fact that we had lost our oldest son to pneumonia made us especially aware of the seriousness of high fever for a small child.

We had left Germany for good. Germany: the land of our youth, with wonderful memories of home and family life on the farm; the land of our hopes and dreams; the land where I had joined the army in peace time, not realizing what that would lead to; the land where we had left our firstborn behind on that little hill where his coffin was buried; the land where we struggled with new realities in the process of adjusting to the postwar era; the land that Ernusch and I were not sorry to leave behind. We were ready to begin anew.

When the last light from the German lighthouse disappeared into the night, we embraced without shedding any tears. Before we retired for the night, my name was suddenly called over the speaker system, asking me to come to the main office on the *Beaverbrae*—the first personal call in the English language. When I arrived at the office I was presented with a bouquet of roses with a farewell wish from the Magnussen family. I was deeply touched and reminded of the special bond which had developed from the first hour in Dörphof with that heroic elderly lady, who had lost her three sons in action during the war. It was a *leb wohl* from Germany.

Life on board the *Beaverbrae* soon became routine. Alex's condition stabilized after he received medication, but I became ill with a kidney infection. That made things more difficult for Ernusch. She was often left alone to look after the boys. A young man, perhaps 17 years old, befriended our boys and helped a great deal, especially at mealtime.

When we were on the high seas an incident occurred which involved another young man. While playing on the steel bars, he had fallen and hit his head on a protruding piece of steel. He died instantly. Since the *Beaverbrae* was sailing under the British flag, the ship's captain was responsible for following their customs for burial at sea. The passengers were mainly German-speaking, so the captain had a hard time finding someone who could officiate at the burial ceremony in English.

On board was a large group of evangelically oriented emigrants who had attracted attention because of their group singing. They were approached, but their spiritual leader refused to officiate since "he did not know if this young man had been a born-again Christian." I don't know who suggested my name, but I was asked and agreed to help out. My brother Hans, his wife Annchen, Ernusch and I and a few others formed a small choir to help make the ceremony more meaningful. The body of the young man was put into a dark green body bag and placed under the British flag. The choir sang—I don't remember which song—then I read a Bible passage and spoke to the small crowd which had gathered.

The captain followed with his traditional ceremony, reading the passages and performing the necessary formalities. Then the ship stopped for a moment and the crew tilted the stretcher to one side. The flag remained over the body as it slipped almost unnoticed into the ocean. I wrote a letter to the young man's mother in Germany where she had remained—they were "displaced persons" from Hungary—but she never wrote back.

During the voyage we experienced a storm, severe enough to cause seasickness for many passengers. I had some trouble as well, but the rest of the family was not affected.

Our three older boys sometimes played on deck. One day Christoph, who was three, fell on the steel threshold of our cabin. He suffered heavy bleeding from a head wound. A young man carried him to the Red Cross station which was close to our cabin. Ernusch saw the motionless boy, hanging limp over the young man's shoulder. After the experience with death a few days earlier, it was no wonder that she reacted in fear and shock. When I arrived at the Red Cross station, Christoph was no longer unconscious and the doctor assured us there was no reason for great concern. How thankful we were to the Lord that he had protected our boy.

On the morning of May 5 a call was heard on deck, "Land in sight." Not long after that we entered the St. Lawrence River. From there on we had land on both sides. Toward evening we arrived at the Quebec City harbour, but it was too late to disembark.

On May 7 we touched Canadian soil.

IV

Finding a Way of Life in Canada:
Family, Farm and Faith

When we boarded the Beaverbrae, *C.F. Klassen said to me and my brother, Hans, "Boys, when you get to Canada and see the farming there, you will think they are doing everything wrong. Be silent for five years before you speak up. And one more thing, Continue to nourish the sense of family life."*
. . . Six-and-a-half years had passed since then and I was ready to speak in a different arena. I decided to accept the challenge of becoming congregational chairman of our home church.

34. From East to West

Every year we observe May 7 as a special day. But on that day in 1951 we were in no mood to celebrate. After Christoph recovered from his head wound, he developed a high temperature and Alex was also ill. After disembarking from the *Beaverbrae,* we entered a huge hall which was used for handling and processing the large number of immigrants. After we completed the immigration procedure our luggage arrived and customs officials asked us to open every piece.

All our wooden boxes had been packed in Germany under customs' supervision, then secured with steel bands. We had documents to prove it, but the Canadian officials insisted on checking all our belongings. We had no tools to pry open the steel bands and the train which was taking us west was scheduled to leave very shortly. We used the little broken English we knew to try and explain our predicament, but without success. Suddenly my brother Hans heard one of the customs officers speaking French. So he switched to the French language, which he had learned fairly well while stationed in France during the war. Immediately, they became friendly and we were not required to open one piece of luggage. They even helped us transport our belongings to the train. What a sudden change in attitude only because we knew their language.

In a short while everything we owned was on board the train and we left Quebec City, heading west. We planned to stop in Winnipeg for a visit with the two Kröker families. They wanted to get to know their niece Annchen's family and also the Siegfried and Erna Bartel family, the people whom they had sponsored to come to Canada.

The train left Quebec City toward evening. When daylight approached, we looked out of the windows of our comfortable roomette to see our new homeland. The woods in northern Quebec and Ontario reminded me of the seemingly endless expanse of swampy woods in Russia. We had thought that Canada was the land of farms, but that whole day we did not see a single farm, only woods. The telephone poles along the railway tracks looked just like the mid-sized trees we saw in the woods, unlike in Germany where they were very even in size and shape. Was this rugged land to be the country with a future for us?

A few hours before we arrived in Winnipeg the scene changed. There were actually farms all along the railway track. In Winnipeg the Kröker families awaited us at the station. German-speaking people embraced us, taking us under their wings. The warmth of their hospitality was so overwhelming that we were tempted to stay and settle there. In addition, it was springtime and the soil in the fields reminded us of farming at home in West Prussia.

When we discussed the farming opportunities for immigrants in Canada, both Onkel Krökers thought that starting out would be easier in British Columbia. Furthermore, Onkel Rempel was expecting us to come to B.C. where he had made all the arrangements. So off we went on the train going even further west. The second day of the journey Alex again developed a high temperature. The conductor made arrangements for a doctor to see our sick child at the next stop. He gave him penicillin and his condition improved temporarily.

As we travelled westward through the mountains we asked the same questions as we had on our trip through northern Quebec and Ontario. The beauty of the Rockies was impressive, but until only a few hours away from our destination we kept wondering: Where are the farms? The first town we saw was Agassiz. It never dawned on us that that would become home to us----our Canadian home.

Onkel and Tante Rempel gave us a warm welcome when we arrived in Mission City. We were a bit taken aback when Tante Rempel made some remark about the amount of luggage we had. Most immigrants before us probably had a lot less.

David and Louise Rempel farmed with their children at the Ridge Top Dairy, approximately five kilometres east of Abbotsford close to the Trans-Canada Highway. Their farm was one of the most modern ones in the area with nearly 100 milk cows. Onkel Rempel, who operated the farm with his two oldest sons, had a very high profile within the farming community and was held in high regard by business people, banks and real estate agents alike.

When Hans and Annchen contacted him regarding emigration to Canada, he had bought them a farm in Rosedale. They stayed at Rempel's house for only a short time, then moved to their "own" farm. Operating the farm involved milking a whole herd of cows by hand. For us Onkel Rempel had rented a small farm on Dixon Road in Sumas. To furnish the house he took Ernusch and me to Abbotsford where we bought all the furniture we needed to get started for less than $100. After two or three nights with the Rempels, we moved into "our" house.

During our stay at the Rempels we had been preoccupied with Alex who once again developed a very high fever. We went to Dr. Barkman in Abbotsford. He spoke German so we could explain what had happened on our two-week voyage.

Tante Rempel thought we were overly anxious about Alex's health, but the worst time came during the first few days at Dixon Road. Dr. Barkman advised us to give the little boy a bath in lukewarm water for a certain number of minutes, then dry him and put him to bed to sleep. We were so afraid to put that hot little body into lukewarm water, but we followed doctor's orders. He fell asleep, and slept all night, the following day, and the next night. How often Ernusch got up to check if he was still breathing. During that crisis one thought haunted us again and again: Will we have to bury our Siegfried Alexander in this strange land after already having buried our firstborn, Siegfried, in West Prussia? We were so thankful to God that this fear never became a reality. When he awoke early the next morning, the fever had broken and he recovered in a short time.

35. Farming on Our Own

Onkel Rempel not only rented the farm for us, he also bought a herd of 14 cows to set us up in the dairying business. His decisions surpassed all my expectations. I questioned his bold planning and asked him if it wouldn't be advisable for me to work for a local farmer first so I could learn about farming in Canada.

Onkel Rempel replied, "Do you want to farm?" Hearing my convincing, "Yes," he said, "You have to start out with debt. The details of farming you will learn for yourself along the way." That answered my question and removed my apprehensions.

I had heard that Hans and Annchen and their family in Rosedale were having difficulty milking their whole herd by hand. Realizing how difficult it would be for us to do the same, I insisted that a milking machine be installed at Dixon Road before the 14 cows would be moved there.

I said: "Onkel Rempel, no one should ever accuse me of being lazy, but I will *not* milk 14 cows by hand!" I guess Onkel Rempel was perplexed, but he honoured my request and installed a used McCormick milking machine.

A new chapter in our lives began with this sudden responsibility of farming. Although I had learned to milk a cow——that was one requirement to get an agriculture diploma in Germany—I certainly was not an experienced milker. Ernusch had helped with regular milking chores on her parents' farm but handling a milking machine was a totally new experience for both of us. But we were ready and eager to learn. When the first can of milk was full, I took it on a specially built wheelbarrow to the little milk house. There a rotating cooler was placed into the can to keep the milk from spoiling until it was picked up by a truck. Lifting the 100-pound cans on to the milkstand was quite a challenge for me in the beginning.

Besides the dairy cattle we had half an acre of raspberries and about the same area seeded in pole beans. Driving the bean poles into the hard ground taught me the basics of hard physical work in a way I had never before experienced. I used a steel crowbar to make holes for the wooden poles. Since I knew nothing about working gloves I used my elegant leather gloves from Germany. They soon became totally tattered. My soft hands could not stand the rough steel crowbar very long without consequences. Many of the poles in that bean patch bore blood marks from my blisters.

During my years in Dörphof I had to find a delicate balance between a sea of refugees from eastern Germany and an old established society; between the noble lady who represented the previous farm generation and an arrogant farm couple who were interested only in their own well-being; between estate owners and the hard-

We transported the 100-pound milk cans on a specially built wheelbarrow when we began farming on Dixon Road near Sumas in 1951.

Erna was my farming partner during our early years on Dixon Road.

working, dedicated farm workers. After the defeat of the German Army, I had to struggle with being a farmer midst the turmoil which accompanied the total defeat of a country. Such struggles tend to influence personal relationships and the reality of coming to terms with one's own identity.

On Dixon Road we very consciously celebrated our freedom. We had to please Onkel and Tante Rempel but other than that, for that short period of life, our world centred only on our family. Ernusch and I did much of the work together. Despite the difficulties and adjustments, we enjoyed it. Doing the farm chores was actually the first time in our life that we worked so closely as a family. In the morning we went to the barn together, while the boys were still asleep; in the afternoon the baby carriage with Alex accompanied us.

Those early years in Canada were full of surprises and learning. Some things were quite primitive. Doing laundry without a washing machine and carrying the water from a ditch was not an easy task. Sometimes Ernusch could use Tante Rempel's washing machine but, since we had no vehicle, she had to transport all the laundry by bicycle to the Rempels and return the wet loads back to Dixon Road in the carriers in the front and back of the bicycle. On occasion the heavy wet laundry would slip off the carrier and was anything but clean when she got it home. On Sunday morning when all "her men" in the family had clean, well-ironed shirts, no one thought of the tears that had been shed by the mother of our family.

During our only winter on Dixon Road we experienced a variety of hardships. The frost was so intense that the hand pump in the barn, which provided the water supply for our cows, could not be used. We broke a hole in the ice in the ditch and scooped out what we could with a pail. There was only very little water. Half the pail was filled with chunks of ice which I dumped on a pile outside the barn to form a little ice mountain. Milk from the evening had to be taken into the kitchen to prevent it from freezing. The pulsators from the milking machines also had to be brought in so they were operable in the morning.

Since we had none of our own farm machinery to do the field work, the hay harvesting was done with Onkel Rempel's machinery and under his guidance. The first time we used the baler and needed to bring the bales into the barn, Onkel Rempel put seven-year-old Gerd behind the steering wheel of his pick-up truck and told him to drive the truck around the field while we loaded the bales. The truck had a stick shift so Gerd had a hard time reaching the clutch.

Onkel Rempel works the field at the Dixon Road farm with the Farmall H tractor.

During the summer Onkel Rempel liked to spoil our boys and us by bringing along ice-cream when he came to the farm. The thrifty Tante Rempel thought he was overdoing it. That ended his treats. In other areas they were both generous. For example, when we started our own household, without a refrigerator or a deep-freeze, Rempels always supplied us with meat. Onkel Rempel said they had butchered one calf for us, which lasted for the year we lived on Dixon Road.

Gerd and Reinhard started school in September 1951. I still remember standing at the driveway with Ernusch and the two little ones, Christoph and Alex, as we watched the two walking hand in hand to catch the school bus. Both boys, wearing their European coats with knapsacks on their backs, walked into the unknown. It turned out to be an unknown alright. German-speaking girls on the bus (from the Kehler family who had picked raspberries on our farm) helped them out at the first stop. That was actually the wrong school but they stayed there for the rest of our time in Sumas.

Gerd was always very protective of Reinhard. One day he came home and said to Ernusch, "Now they won't laugh and make fun of us any more." He had taken steps to deal with the situation. Our boys always took along a glass bottle of milk for lunch. Gerd had hit one of the boys, who always teased Reinhard, over the head with his knapsack and had broken his empty milk bottle. According to Gerd, that action should solve the problem.

In Canada we had some difficulties with our first names. At the Sumas school they changed Gerd to George. Onkel Rempel made the arrangements for my first bank loan to pay for the 14 cows under the name, Fred Bartel. For the first year in Canada I signed all documents and cheques with that name. Next year when I went in to sign for another loan, I changed back to Siegfried. The bank manager in Agassiz asked to see my passport and informed me that it was actually illegal to sign Fred Bartel. Gerd returned to his original name in Agassiz as well.

During the winter months a large group of West Prussian Mennonites arrived in the Fraser Valley. My sister Gertraut had come shortly after we did and had joined us on Dixon Road for the raspberry picking season. My sister Ruth, cousin Ernst, Hans-Peter Bartel and cousin Hans Andres with their families all arrived by the end of 1951.

In early spring of 1952 it became known that my parents would join us in Canada. At the same time Onkel Rempel decided that we should not continue to rent a farm for the second year. He began looking for a farm to buy, first a small one but later suggested a larger operation. My brother Walter, who had spent some time working on Onkel Rempel's farm and at various other jobs, was interested in going into farming as well.

While he was searching for the right farming property, Onkel Rempel got in touch with E.J. Meilicke and Sons in Vancouver, a company with which he had some previous dealings. The Agassiz hop yard was on their real estate listings. They suggested to Onkel Rempel that we should consider that property. Hans Andres was also interested in farming and had asked Onkel Rempel for advice. Since he remembered his close friendship with Hans's parents in Schroop, Onkel Rempel suggested that we include Hans in the purchase. In early March my brother Walter, cousin Hans Andres and I made our first trip to Agassiz to see the property. We all liked it. A new era began with our plans to buy the Agassiz hop yard.

36. The Bartel-Andres Partnership

We were ready to begin a new chapter in our lives in the beautiful farming area 100 kilometres east of Vancouver. Access to Agassiz was possible only on the north shore of the Fraser River via Mission City on a partially steep mountain road, or on the Rosedale-Agassiz ferry which crossed the Fraser River. The ferry traffic was at best an inconvenience; at worst, especially in high water time in May and June and during the winter months, quite unpredictable. In the late 1920s and 1930s there had been a Mennonite Brethren settlement there, but the isolation factor had influenced the settlers to move away, most of them to the Yarrow area. When we arrived in Agassiz, only three Mennonite families remained: the Engbrechts, the Neufeldts and Heinz and Ortrud Schmidt. None of them were Mennonite Brethren.

The quality of the soil in the Agassiz farming area ranged from top quality adjacent to the Fraser River and north of the railway tracks, to poorer quality toward Harrison Hot Springs and the lower land west of Agassiz. The 175 acres we were buying from the B.C. Hop Company was mostly top grade soil.

The first time Onkel Rempel and I looked at the property in March 1952 we spent a great deal of time going over the fields. The Hop Company had installed an underground irrigation system for the hop fields and wanted to salvage the pipes. Workers were just in the

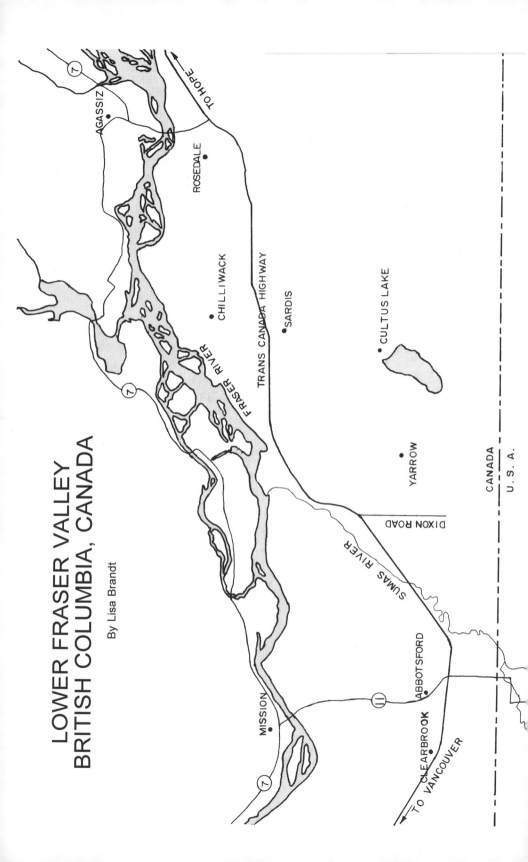

LOWER FRASER VALLEY
BRITISH COLUMBIA, CANADA

By Lisa Brandt

process of digging them out. With those ditches all over the fields, we were able to evaluate the soil easily and were both highly impressed.

There were four residences on the property. When I asked Onkel Rempel if I could have a look at the main house, he was not very pleased.

"You are making your living from the land and not from the houses," he said. So I spent only a few minutes in it and didn't have a chance to look into any of the other three houses.

Onkel Rempel was a successful farmer and a very respected organizer. After seeing the Agassiz Hop Yard property, he made all the necessary arrangements without much consultation with us. There was no time to lose if we were to buy the farm and occupy it for the spring seeding season. None of the papers were signed by the three of us before we moved on to the farm. Onkel Rempel as guarantor must have done all of that. The sale agreement, which we only signed on June 3, 1952, showed that interest payments were calculated to begin on April 22. Purchase price of the property was $43,875. According to the "Agreement of Sale," $6,000 of that was to be paid by December 1952, the remaining in monthly payment of $450 at 6 percent interest.

There were various reasons for Onkel Rempel's enthusiasm about the Agassiz hop yard deal. First of all, the soil was excellent and the price low compared to farms on the south side of the Fraser River. Then, the opportunity of bringing three of us—the Hans Andres family, Walter and me with family—into one operation made it considerably easier for him to take care of all of us. He took the position, and rightly so, that it was a three-man farming operation. Also, there were enough houses on the property for his plan of including my parents, who were expected to come to Canada shortly. A further advantage was that brother Hans and his family in Rosedale were close by, just across the Fraser River.

Onkel Rempel was shrewd enough to realize that, because farms in that area were relatively low in price, he would be able to find a suitable farm in the vicinity to start off Ruth (my sister) and Ernst Schroeder. Another assurance he had was that "his Bartels," with whom he had by now developed a close relationship, even a friendship, would meet the challenge of managing this undertaking.

Some members of his home church, Yarrow Mennonite Brethren, criticized him for settling the Prussian emigrants too far away from a Mennonite church. He brushed aside that objection with, "The

Bartels do not fit into the *Ansiedlung*" (the German term used for newly established farm villages). In addition, he knew that Vati would provide solid spiritual leadership and nurture when he arrrived.

Onkel Rempel never forgot that he had found a home in Reich-felde after his time of service in the "White Army" during the revolution in Russia. He was one of the "Constantinopler" (White Army soldiers who crossed over to Constantinople, Turkey, after the victory of the Red Army), one of the homeless ones who had found a new home in Reichfelde and had become a friend of our father. When he emigrated to Canada with his family in 1927, our father and Ernusch's uncle paid for his voyage to Canada. Now he had an opportunity to give special meaning to his "thank you" to Heinrich Bartel.

On April 22, possession day, the three of us began a cooperative venture as "Bartel and Andres:" three equal partners but in many ways very different. Walter was in his early twenties, physically strong with lots of experience in hard work; not married but with education in agriculture as *staatlich geprüfter Landwirt* (state-educated agriculturalist) with a college diploma, the same as the other partners. Hans Andres was married to Lore. They had three boys——their only

In 1952 with farming partners cousin Hans Andres and brother Walter.

daughter, Ann, was born later. He had valuable experience as manager of large farms before the war, but without Walter's physical strength nor experience in doing heavy physical work. The last two points on Hans—not much physical strength and minimal experience in hard work—applied to me as well. One difference in my background was that I had managed a farm operation for six years after the war before we emigrated to Canada. We had four boys at that time and the oldest two—Gerd age 9 and Reinhard age 7—were beginning to be helpers on the farm, the same as the Andres' boys.

Hans and Lore with their boys were the first to move to Agassiz. On April 23, 1952, we moved our cows from Dixon Road. Gerd and I accompanied the truck driver with the cattle. Ernusch with the other boys went with Onkel Rempel in his truck which carried all our other belongings.

The condition of the four houses on the farm varied. Right on the yard was the house where the hop yard administrator had lived and where the office had been located. It was in good shape and had a full bathroom and a heating system with a wood and coal furnace in the basement. The upstairs had one bedroom and open space. Not far from the manager's house close to Tuyttens Road was the large boarding house where farm workers employed by the B.C. Hop Company had lived. That house had not been used nor cleaned after the 1948 flood. Although the house had no insulation, it was very spacious. The upstairs had many rooms but had no heat supply and the stairs were shaky. Only the downstairs, which had running water and a full bathroom, was livable. The house close to the mountains, where the Andres family moved, was very small but had been kept in fairly good condition. The fourth dwelling was in an area where all the cabins for the hop pickers were located. It was a nice looking, small house without insulation, running water or bathroom.

When the partners moved to Agassiz, one contentious issue developed: Who would live in the hopyard manager's house and who would move into the boarding house? My sister Gertraut was coming with us to Agassiz to live with Walter and to take care of my parents when they arrived in Canada. Ernusch and I suggested that the four of them should stay in the manager's house and we would move into the boarding house, but Onkel Rempel decided differently. When Ernusch drove to Agassiz with him, she pleaded with tears in her eyes, but Onkel Rempel had made up his mind.

When they began to unload boxes, he said to her, "Ihr wohnt hier" (You will live here [in the farm manger's house]). As we lead the cows off the cattle truck I walked over to Ernusch who was sitting on one of our large packing boxes, crying.

She said to me, "Hier werde ich nie lachen können" (Here I will never be able to laugh again).

During our time in Dörphof we constantly had needed to adjust to other people like the Magnussen women, the Dr. Francke situation and six different parties in one farmhouse. Despite all the hardships of coping with the new world at Dixon Road, we had experienced "heaven on earth" as a family unit. For Ernusch the change to living in such close contact with relatives, and apparently for a long time to come, loomed like a heavy cloud on the horizon. Although by now her overall relationship to the Bartel family was very good, she was apprehensive about the closeness of the new community. Ever since our engagement in 1938 I had tried to help Ernusch overcome her inferiority complex which she felt mainly because she had less formal education than the members of our family. Becoming part of the Heinrich Bartel Reichfelde family had frightened her because she came from a family that had operated a much smaller farm and had a somewhat different lifestyle.

In setting up the "Agassiz adventure," Onkel Rempel apparently had made up his mind that I would act as leader within the farming partnership. It was his decision alone that we move into the farm manager's house. During the years 1951-56 when he was guarantor for our farm, he would discuss all issues relating to farm management with me personally. That caused some conflict in my relationship with my partners.

Making the arrangements regarding the herd was an even greater challenge than allocating the housing. There was a big hip-roof barn on the yard with facilities only for horses. We had to tie up the cows with ropes in the horse stalls. The milking machine had to be installed the first evening. We were fortunate that Walter was such an excellent mechanic. Since there were no fenced-in fields on the farm, our first recorded expense was an electric fence for $19.93.

At first the little pumphouse was used as a milkhouse for cooling the fresh milk. That was the only place where we could connect the cooler. To transport the milk cans to the pumphouse we used the boys' little play wagon. The first hop pickers' cabin we moved became a milkhouse on the east side of the barn.

Remodelling the horse barn into a cow barn needed to be done in a hurry because we had to enlarge the herd extensively. Even though we had no cash on hand to buy cattle, Onkel Rempel made arrangements with his friend, Mr. Klontz, a cattle dealer from Abbotsford. He sent us 33 cows so that the amount of milk for shipment was increased substantially. Only after approximately four years did we begin paying interest on the balance. Similar financial arrangements were made by Onkel Rempel with Mr. Anderson, the McCormick dealer from Vancouver. A few days after we moved to Agassiz, a Farmall H tractor arrived. That was followed by a corn planter, a plow, harrows and some other machinery.

The B.C. Hop Company had sown approximately 30 acres into red clover. The rest of the farm, except for some bushland and pasture by the dike, had to be ploughed and seeded. We signed a contract with a cannery in Mission City and planted 100 acres of sweet corn and six acres of pole beans. With those two crops we were able to make our payment of $6,000 to Meilickes in fall. Besides those fields, approximately 25 acres were seeded into oats and pasture seed so we could get fresh pasture in minimum time.

All the field work had to be done with one tractor. For several weeks we started the tractor on Monday morning and kept it in operation day and night until Saturday midnight. For the first nine months at Agassiz the Farmall H tractor was our only motorized vehicle. We mounted a platform on the back and used it for outings on Sundays.

Ploughing the large fields, preparing the soil for seeding and planting the 100 acres of corn presented extremely difficult challenges. Mistakes were made. The first field of corn had to be planted twice. For the first planting we had put the fertilizer too close to the corn kernels and burned the sprouting seed. In those days the corn was not sprayed for weeds, so cultivating the fields, especially when the corn was just coming up, took many hours. Over the years we developed quite an art in growing corn and for a number of years the three of us became the Agassiz Corn Kings in a local community competition.

Every year we made some adjustments in the distribution of different crops. We grew pole beans only in 1952. The next two years we had larger fields of green peas and did additional threshing of green peas on contract for a Chilliwack cannery. That arrangement allowed us to employ many of our friends and others. In spring 1953 we had planted four acres of raspberries. The berries turned out to be a good source of additional income so we later enlarged the field to five acres. Less successful was our chicken business which we phased out after one year.

For the most part we experienced success in farming during those years, but we also experienced serious setbacks. In the fall of 1952 we had bought 12 very nice Holstein heifers from Mr. Klontz. One day we noticed there was something wrong with the younger stock. We got them all home and called the veterinarian. The heifers had pastured in an area of bush where we found poisonous powder which had been used by the hop yard for spraying the hops. We lost seven of the 12 heifers. The loss was not only the purchase money for the seven cattle, but also the resulting curtailment in our milk quota and a drastic drop in milk production at a time when the amount of the milk cheque was extremely important. The other major set-back to improving our herd was the presence of brucellosis. Many of the cows could not carry their pregnancies to full term which meant a major down-turn in building up our herd.

During those early years we were spared any fatal accidents, although some serious incidents did occur. The first one happened when Walter and our nephew Werner Bartel were on their way home from Mission City with an empty truck late one evening. Walter was blinded by an oncoming car and went off the road. The truck rolled down the embankment to the bottom of the bay and landed on one side. The young trees on the slope had prevented the truck from rolling down dangerously fast. Walter and Werner were able to climb out through the free door and came home unhurt. A more critical

Baling hay during our farming operation as Bartel-Andres partnership.

incident happened when Walter was doing custom work baling hay. His pant leg became caught in the tractor's power take-off shaft. Some skin and muscle tissue were torn off his Achilles tendon and heel. Luckily none of the tendons were seriously damaged, but a weakness remained even after the foot had healed. A number of years later, Reinhard was on the tractor pulling the manure spreader along the dike when the right front tire had a blow-out. He lost control and the tractor rolled down the embankment. He jumped off and only his rubber boots were caught by the overturned tractor. He was able to free his foot, unhurt, out of his boot and walk home.

During the threshing season in 1954 we experienced some excitement with a romantic love story. Lore Andres' brother, Morry Bartels, who lived in Washington state, had helped Sylvia, his bride-to-be, come from Europe to Canada. She stayed with Hans and Lore. Lore's nephew, Gerd Weller, was also living with them while he worked on our farm. It did not take long before that handsome young man impressed Sylvia more than did the older, business-like Morry. The day the young couple informed Hans and Lore that they planned to get married, they were asked to leave the house. In the evening they appeared at our doorstep, but we were not willing to take them in. So they moved into the Agassiz Hotel. They later became a happy couple.

We made many close friends in Agassiz. Among them were the three Mennonite families which had remained there from an earlier settlement group. The Cornelius Neufeldts were most helpful during our new beginnings. Onkel Neufeldt and his Ford tractor assisted us in many situations. After his wife died suddenly in December 1953, he worked on our farm off and on for many years. Another couple was Henry and Ortrud Schmidt. Henry was an electrician by trade. Then there were the Engbrechts who had one of the nicest looking farms in Agassiz.

Our first contact with Mr. Engbrecht happened in a way that Ernusch will never forget. A few months after we moved in, the three farming partners had to go with Onkel Rempel to the Meilicke office in Vancouver to sign the agreement for buying our farm. June is high-water season so the ferry was not running and we were stranded in Rosedale. When milking time came Ernusch, Gertraut and Lore had to milk the cows. Ernusch had some experience in milking, especially from our time on Dixon Road, but she had never used the milking machines on her own. When they started the process, the teat-cups kept falling off. The women were at a point of desperation when a man walked into the barn, greeting them in the German language. He had heard that the newcomers were of German stock and he wanted to find out who they were. After the first few words of greeting, Ernusch asked him for help. He looked at the machines and smiled. The air hoses were connected the wrong way—that was the only problem.

By far the most significant people during our early years in Agassiz were my parents. They arrived from Enkenbach, Germany, in July 1952. Although they very much enjoyed their position as houseparents in the Mennonite Old Folks Home there, they wanted to be closer to most of their children who had emigrated to Canada. Vatchen was also very eager to join three of his sons who were farming again. Onkel Rempel had offered to pay for their voyage to Canada and to sign all guarantees necessary for an aging couple.

Tante Rempel and Muttchen had never been very close. Their strained relationship had begun when Muttchen came to Reichfelde as our stepmother. It was then that Tante Rempel and Plati's leading role in the household came to an end. Tante Rempel, a classic workaholic with extremely strong practical orientations, had very little in common with Muttchen who nurtured her poetic gifts and her interest in writing and maintaining extensive correspondence. In many ways they were as different as any two people could be, in spite of the fact that they had the same roots in a strong faith.

Farming with Vatchen was very enjoyable and we had several wonderful years together. His health was much better here in B.C. than it had been in West Prussia. His love for dairy farming was also revived. That wonderful man, who had not worked with his hands since he was young, became active in driving the tractor, feeding calves and helping with the chores.

During the years of farming as "Bartel and Andres" our working relationship had its ups and downs. All in all it was very harmonious and we were just as close friends at the end as on the day the partnership began. We accepted each other's work as of equal importance and had no differences of opinion on financial matters. I must admit that the peaceful atmosphere sometimes was tested by the presence of our children. As parents we usually defend our own children's behaviour and the three partners differed in their philosophy of raising children. Situations arose when a great deal of tolerance and self-control were needed to overcome times of tension.

The Bartel and Andres farming partnership lasted until January 1, 1956, a total of three years and nine months, when Hans and Lore went out on their own. By that time we had approximately 60 milk cows and a fair number of young stock.

Vati was quite concerned about the process of dividing up the herd, two-thirds and one-third. I remember well my reply to him: "Vatchen, if there will be any problems, then I am the one to be blamed." The three of us sat down on a few bales of hay in the barn and started dividing the herd, up to the youngest calf. At the end of the process we were all satisfied.

37. The Bartel Brothers Operation

On January 1, 1956, Hans Andres started to milk his own herd while Walter and I operated our part of the farm as Bartel Brothers. The official legal separation between us and Hans Andres was May 23, 1956, when the Prudential Insurance Co. gave us separate mortgages and we paid off Meilicke Brothers. Walter had been married in summer 1955 to Elfriede Schmidt from Germany. Our sister Gertraud, who had run the household for Walter and looked after my parents, moved to Vancouver to find employment. Elfriede stepped in as *Hausfrau* and partner in the farming operation.

After dividing up the herd we took steps to increase the number of milk cows on our Bartel Brothers farm. We bought a number of registered Holsteins from the Agassiz Experimental Farm—our first purchase of purebred cattle.

With my Holstein dairy herd in Agassiz.

Vati at his desk in Enkenbach before he and Muttchen joined us in Canada in 1952.

To operate our farm efficiently we bought another tractor—a McCormick Super A—because Hans Andres had taken the Farmall C into his operation. During the building of the Agassiz-Rosedale Bridge one of the construction companies left a McCormick W6 tractor on the bank of the river. We bought it for a small amount of money but it required many parts before Walter could rebuild it completely. All the machinery for making silage was shared by us and our brother Hans in Rosedale.

By that time our sons were getting into the teenage years. They were not always very easy on my brother, Walter. As our master mechanic and the person responsible for maintaining the machinery, he expected that the tractors should be treated with some respect. Certainly that did not always happen.

Those years of farming as Bartel Brothers were very happy times for my father. He saw his sons as respected and successful farmers in the community. Furthermore, he enjoyed seeing us follow in his footsteps in the dairy business. In July 1957 he travelled to the Mennonite World Conference in Karlsruhe, Germany. He died there suddenly on August 14. What a loss for the whole family but mainly for Muttchen. Vatchen was buried in Enkenbach, close to the Old Folks' Home where he had served as its first administrator. My sister-in-law Annchen had accompanied him to Germany so only she, my sister Magdalena and husband Paul Schneiderreit, and our brother Heinz-Otto and wife Annemarie represented the immediate family at the funeral.

The shock to Muttchen was indescribable. That great woman, who had been on the threshold of death many times, suddenly was a widow for the second time in her life. The grave of her first husband lay in distant West Prussia. He had been her sunshine when she was young. Now she had lost Vatchen, her husband of 37 years, with whom she had walked hand in hand into old age.

Before Vatchen left on his trip to Karlsruhe, he had heard that the farmer with land next to ours was thinking of selling the farm. Vati suggested that Walter buy it and sell me his part of Bartel Brothers.

On October 1, 1958, Walter and Elfriede started out on their own farm. By then our herd was as large as it had been two years earlier when we separated from Hans Andres. We divided the cattle herd in half, but I bought back a number of cows since half would have been too large for Walter's 40-acre farm. I took over the remaining payments on the Bartel Brothers operation.

38. Our Six Sons

Although farming in Agassiz absorbed much of our time and energy, we also found great joy and satisfaction in family life. Raising our boys was a joy for both Ernusch and me. Despite some concerns at various times, we never shed a tear over their behaviour. During our second year in Agassiz, another son was added to the family. Dietrich was born in October 1953. Our family was complete when Martin was born in August 1957. After his birth Ernusch took longer to recover and get back to full strength. Vatchen had died on August 14, only a week before Martin was born. From Karlsruhe we received his last letter to us dated August 5. It closed with the words:

. . . my greeting to both of you. My beloved Ernusch, I commend you to the grace of God. The Lord give you strength to get over the difficult hours. May he give you a healthy child---maybe a girl?!

It was not to be. Dr. G. Enns, our family physician, looked disappointed when the baby was born.

Ernusch asked him, "Is the child healthy?"

"Yes," he said, "but it's a boy."

Ernusch was immediately cheerful and accepted the fact that she would be the only female in the family for quite some time to come. Now we had six sons—Gerd, the eldest, was 14. Ernusch had her hands full: cooking and baking for all of us, getting all the work clothes and Sunday clothes ready for when we needed them, taking care of everyone's personal concerns, acting as a gracious hostess for the extended family, being a wonderful wife. And then there was the garden—a hobby for both of us.

One of the difficult realities was that there was hardly any cash available, not even to buy clothing. During the Bartel and Andres farming arrangement, each family got $30 a month for personal needs. The basic foods like flour, milk, butter and meat were supplied by the farm, but how could anyone manage with $30 for family needs? The situation changed little when we farmed as Bartel Brothers. I remember going to a Finance Company in Chilliwack to borrow $200 to have money for Christmas. At the bank both our business and private accounts were stretched to the limit.

The boys often had to stay home from school to work on the farm. (When Alex graduated from grade 12 he took out all his report cards and added up the days he had been absent from school. The total amounted to about one school year.) Whenever possible we tried not to have the boys do morning chores in the barn on school days. We placed great importance on being punctual at the breakfast table so we could be together for breakfast and daily family devotions.

As a couple, we continued the German tradition of having the main meal at noon. When the boys came home from school they had their hot meal. If possible, Ernusch and I kept them company by having coffee before starting the evening chores. We always tried to have the chores done by 6:30 or 7:00 so we could be free for the evening, often for meetings or for the boys and their activities.

Ernusch and I were brought up in the European family tradition, mostly a very harmonious environment, but the strap was used for punishment on occasions when the parents felt the need. We followed

With our six sons at Christmas 1957 (from oldest to youngest, right to left): Gerd, Reinhard, Christoph, Alex; (in front): Martin on Erna's lap and Dietrich

the admonition in Proverbs 13:24: "He who spares the rod hates his son, but he who loves him is diligent to discipline him." We did not use the rod very often and certainly never in anger or in great haste. I remember sometimes weeping with the boys when I used the rubber hose in the milkhouse.

When unacceptable behaviour had reached its limit, we often used the phrase, "The measure is almost full and running over." Martin told us later that, as a small boy, he had tried to find that measure, thinking that we actually used a measuring cup to evaluate when it was time for punishment.

Despite financial strain, we tried hard to make life on the farm a joyful time for our sons. With my longtime love for horses, we wanted to give our boys the opportunity to develop the same interest. We bought the first riding horse in 1960 and later had up to seven horses. I remember Walter (my brother) saying, "For every 10 cows you have one horse." As on most farms, we also enjoyed our dogs.

In the late 1950s we started skiing with the boys at Manning Park at a time when the main language spoken on the ski hill was German.

We bought the first pair of skis at a second-hand store in Vancouver for $2.00. Once Gerd was able to drive, we eventually stayed home, leaving the sport to the boys.

The first boat we bought was built by Henry (Jurgen) Bartel and his friend. It was too small for waterskiing. When Gerd and Reinhard became active with church young people, we bought a good-sized boat with a motor powerful enough for that sport. The whole family enjoyed it for many years.

Farming with three, later two partners, allowed us to take time off on Sundays as well as for vacations. The first summer holiday we took was in August 1955. We travelled to the Okanagan Valley with our friend Carl-Heinz von Muehldorfer at a time when we did not yet have our own vehicle. Carl Heinz—Charlie we called him—was a friend of our friend, Christoph Nehring. He came from Germany in May 1954. Our house became his Canadian home until he got married.

Ernusch and I were very strict with the boys regarding the use of the German language. We wanted to preserve our mother tongue so they would be able to use it as adults. In school the boys spoke only English, but we insisted on German as the language we spoke in our family home. That was not easy, especially in later years. I remember the boys had to write 100 lines as punishment for speaking English in the house: "Ich soll im Haus deutsch sprechen" (I must speak German in the house). Later the boys were thankful for our insistence that they speak German. They have used it often in their work and study settings.

Already as a youngster, Gerd exhibited maturity beyond his years. His influence on his brothers over the years was exceptional. Reinhard looked up to him for guidance and protection, finding security in the unfamiliar Canadian environment. This special relationship was to be an enduring one. It was a great help to us as parents that the older sons became role models for the younger ones.

Ernusch and I were always concerned about our boys' friends, knowing knew how influential peers can be. Generally the boys had two kinds of friends: one group from school or neighbourhood, the other from church or relative circles. Chrisoph's best friend was Ivan Walker with whom he shared a love for the outdoors. That long-lasting friendship affected our whole family, especially during the time of Ivan's struggle with cancer, ultimately with death. Christoph was the one who had the hardest time accepting and tolerating school rules. Across from the school yard was a small butcher shop operated by Jim Scott. Jim, a hunter about 10 years older than Christoph, became his friend. One afternoon I went to do business at the butcher shop where Christoph often spent noon hours helping Jim. That day he had unloaded his frustrations on Jim. Christoph's relationship to Mr. Curley, the vice-principal, was at its lowest point.

He told Jim that noon hour: "If I would not have been brought up like I have, I would have hit him right between the eyes with my fist." How happy I was that his upbringing and the example of his family were bearing fruit.

Alex developed stronger ties to his friends in Sunday school and later in the church youth group. Those connections to the home church continued during his time at the University of British Columbia. Eventually Martha Goertzen from church became his life partner. Christoph, Alex and Martin were the three boys who found their wives within Eden Mennonite, our home church.

Dietrich discovered his love for music early in life. One day when he was nine years old, we were all returning home from a church wedding. As is custom, wedding receptions were held in the lower auditorium of the church. The children usually found their own entertainment in the adjacent Sunday school rooms. There Dietrich had discovered a piano. In the car going home, he enthusiastically told us that he had been able to play the melodies from one of the records which we had often played in our home. Ernusch and I looked at each other. We both enjoyed classical music and listened to many records. But we now knew that we had to buy a piano. That's what we did, even though we had a hard time making payments.

Dietrich became a diligent piano student, waking up the whole family at 6:00 a.m. sharp with his practising—except on Saturdays and Sundays. His brothers objected to 6 a.m. wake-up time on Saturday. Besides that, they were sometimes critical that he "had to practise" while they were required to do chores in the barn. But that practising paid off. Later, when he went to university in Vancouver, the highly acclaimed organist and teacher, Hugh McLean, took him on as his student. The direction for his future was set.

Ernusch and I observed that development with great joy. It had not always been that way. Dietrich's circle of friends at school were not exactly consistent with our standards and goals. They were highly intelligent but found school work unchallenging. During his time in Grade 11 and 12, when the use of drugs became more prevalent, we were especially concerned. Both alcohol and drugs increased their hold on some within that group. At the University of British Columbia Dietrich found a clear direction for his professional goal. Equally important, within the circle of Inter-Varsity Christian Fellowship he found his wonderful life partner, Jocelyn.

Martin, our youngest, also started piano lessons. He was never as keen about practising as Dietrich was, but when it came to music festival time, he often did quite well. Mrs. Wilson, their piano teacher, always claimed that he was just as musical as Dietrich was. At one festival Dietrich had to share a trophy with Martin.

Martin loved his older brother Christoph in a very special way. At that time we sometimes thought that the two together would eventually run our farm. How differently things actually turned out.

Dietrich's ability in practical things was, at one time or another, questioned by all his brothers. One time a prong of the fork with which he was working got stuck in his hand. Another time he fell off a horse that was grazing, not even moving, and ended up with a broken arm. A more serious incident happened when I was unloading hay with Dietrich. When the tractor began to pull up the forklift, Dietrich's left hand became caught between the pulleys and the steel cable. When I grabbed his hand to pull it out, both my right hand *and* his left hand were injured. We jumped into our station wagon and I drove with my left hand. Between us was a towel with my bleeding right hand and his injured left hand. The tendons which were cut on my little finger never totally healed. Dietrich's injury was not as severe.

Family life in Agassiz was very beautiful. We had our struggles with the pressure of farm work and with personal concerns, but the harmony within the family was wonderful. The boys never had a serious fight, at least none that I was aware of.

I am sure that the relationship between Ernusch and me influenced the family atmosphere. Our opinions on some issues certainly differed, but on matters of principle we always presented a united front. The boys tried various ways of approaching the members of our team, depending on where they could more likely expect approval. If, for example, Christoph at age 16 was planning to go up North for a hunting trip with the little mini-Austin, he certainly would not go to Ernusch for permission. If Dietrich wanted "time off" from the barn chores to practise for the piano competition, he knew he would have an excellent advocate in Mutti. Above all, we tried hard to be fair with each one.

The boys felt the freedom to offer their perspective on family matters. Our system was open but clearly patriarchal. Some of our methods of dealing with young sons were probably not that common in other households. For instance, none of our sons owned a motor vehicle before they got married, but we did supply them with a car at our expense, even through college and university. It was actually a package deal, a compensation for the work they did on the farm during their school years. The oldest three spent their first year after graduation from high school working on the farm without pay or, as in the case of Gerd, working in Bob Grosz's machine shop and handing over the cheque to the family account. That did not apply to Alex and Dietrich. They were deducted $3,000 each from the first inheritance funds that we distributed. All of those questions were openly discussed and understood by everyone.

The spiritual nurture of our sons was always extremely important to us. We were thankful when an Inter-School Christian Fellowship (ISCF) group was formed in the Agassiz High School. Gerd was influential in establishing that group and became their second president. There were no teacher sponsors available so Bob Grosz, manager of a mechanic shop for small motors, became the sponsor. All our sons, except Reinhard who attended Grade 11 and 12 in Chilliwack, were local presidents of ISCF in Agassiz.

When we moved from Sumas to Agassiz in 1952 we realized with some regret that our children would not be able to attend the private high school, Mennonite Educational Institute (MEI), in Clearbrook. We simply lived too far away. In Agassiz they learned to be different than the majority of Mennonite young people. I believe that fact contributed to their development as strong yet uniquely different personalities.

39. Church Life in Agassiz

When we first arrived in British Columbia, we regularly attended the Mennonite Brethren Church in Yarrow with the Rempels. Church life in Canada impressed us immensely. I remember the wonderful experience on our first Sunday there. Never before had I heard such powerful congregational singing—all in the German language and that in an English-speaking country. Sunday school for adults was something new for us. We very much enjoyed learning from Johann Harder, pastor of the church. But we encountered our first discrimination in Canada right there at church. Since we were not baptized by immersion we were not welcome at the Lord's

Supper. My sister Gretel, who was married to Abraham Harder, brother of the pastor, had arrived in Canada from Paraguay. They were invited to the Lord's table but we were not.

Those of us who settled in Agassiz were deeply concerned about the spiritual welfare of our group. Hans and Annchen, who lived across the river in Rosedale, attended the East Chilliwack Mennonite Church on Prest Road. However, that was not an option for us because we did not have a car or truck. The Harrison Gospel Chapel, an English-speaking Mennonite Brethren mission church, was also not feasible. Hardly anyone knew English well enough to be able to follow a sermon in that language.

We decided to meet in various homes for Sunday morning worship. When my parents arrived, Vatchen automatically became the spiritual leader of our group. After we bought our three-ton truck in summer 1953, we often went to East Chilliwack for services, picking up the Hans Bartel family in Rosedale on the way. The addition of several more families that year made the group large enough for us to organize formally. A meeting was held on December 13, 1953, to which Ältester A.A. Harder, teacher at the Bible School and member of the B.C. Conference Missions Committee, had been invited.

We agreed to hold regular church services in homes until we could find "a suitable room with low rent." Sunday school would be held before the service. The B.C. Conference would send a minister each Sunday, although the group was considered a project of the Canadian Conference. Heinrich Bartel (Vatchen) was elected unanimously as spokesperson for the group.

In February 1954 we were able to rent a house for our services. The Conference of Mennonites in B.C. promised to pay half the monthly rent of $15.00. Hans-Peter Bartel's minutes indicate that the last offering was held on March 18, 1956. The final rental payment on our Agassiz "church" was made from those funds. By that time every family had a vehicle and the Agassiz-Rosedale Bridge was under construction. Our group was dissolved and the majority joined the East Chilliwack Mennonite Church.

That church was under the leadership of H.H. Neufeld who was very inflexible regarding church rules. Lore Andres had been baptized as a child but had been a member of a Mennonite church in Germany. Nevertheless, the ministers and deacons of the East Chilliwack Mennonite Church were not willing to accept her as a member. So Hans and Lore decided to go to the Harrison Gospel Chapel, a Mennonite Brethren church, where they were willing to accept her as an associate member. Elfriede, my brother Walter's wife, also was baptized as a child. The East Chilliwack Mennonite Church would not accept her as a member without adult baptism, so they joined the Greendale Church in Sardis.

The rest of us, including our parents, joined the East Chilliwack Mennonite Church in the spring of 1957. Ernusch and I have very unpleasant memories of the evening we joined. We were invited to share our spiritual pilgrimage with the members on the same evening as our parents gave their testimony. My parents went in first while Ernusch and I waited in a small entrance of the church. Ernusch was pregnant with Martin at the time. The bench to sit on was only about eight inches wide. It was a very cold evening and the small room had no lights. My parents' testimony was lengthy, detailed and, of course, very interesting, but they were in no hurry. We heard every word but we had to sit in that cold room. We were so upset that, if we would have had our own vehicle, we probably would have left. We did stay and became members.

The constitution of our church included a clear statement on non-resistance and peace. My position when I joined was the same as many other members: we accepted it as a statement in principle but not necessarily out of personal conviction. At the time I could not anticipate that later on in life I would be one of the strongest defenders of the peace position as taught by Jesus.

Soon after we joined the church I was asked to teach a German adult Sunday school class. I accepted the assignment, unaware that some people resented a man who had been a German soldier.

At a congregational meeting one brother, who later became a close friend and supporter, asked: "Is it possible that a previous 'murderer' (referring to my time as a soldier) can teach Sunday school in a Mennonite church?"

I was shocked. I don't even remember how the question was answered. I personally did not respond. Would that question keep haunting me whenever I considered getting involved in church work? It did become a major obstacle when, at the 1957 annual membership meeting, I was elected as congregational chairman for two years. As I struggled with a response I was reminded of C.F. Klassen's advice to me and my brother Hans when we boarded the *Beaverbrae* in Bremerhafen: "Be silent for five years . . . but then speak up according to your convictions." Six-and-a-half years had passed since then and I was ready to speak in a different arena. I decided to accept the challenge and stayed on for two additional terms in 1960 and 1963.

Another obstacle to feeling totally accepted in our church was the fact that we did not speak the Low German dialect. Ernusch has often said that we should have learned Low German before we learned English. I've always maintained that you really cannot learn that language—you have to be born into it.

The years 1960 and 1961 were my most difficult ones regarding board and committee positions in church. At the time I also became a member of the Agassiz-Harrison School Board. Some evenings I came home from church meetings and commented to Ernusch, "When I come home from school board meetings my clothes smell like smoke but at least I can sleep well. After church council meetings my arms are tingling, my nerves are frayed and my sleep is very troubled."

The working relationship among council members was excellent, but less smooth with the pastor. Apparently my predecessor, Brother Dosso, had been an easy-going chairman and had let Pastor Neufeld make all his own decisions. I learned early on that there is a fundamental problem in church politics, a problem that persists in churches today: "What is the responsibility of church council members, who have been prayerfully elected, versus the shepherd, who has been 'anointed' by the Lord?"

Cornelius Fast was an excellent secretary and his minutes were always accurate and helpful. The decision in January 1961 to build a new church—the vote was 66 to 19—sparked a lot of enthusiasm among members. Everyone agreed that something had to be done if the church was to grow. The issue was: remodel or construct a new building?

Shortly after the January decision to build, Isaak Friesen, a church member, offered the congregation a gift of two acres of land if we would relocate to the corner of Chilliwack Central and Broadway where he owned a larger parcel of land. On March 9, 1961, we held a historic meeting to decide whether to accept Friesen's offer. On the first ballot we were short a few votes on the required two-thirds majority. As congregational chairman I did something not found in "Roberts' rules of order." We sang a few songs, had a prayer session and, after a short appeal, I called for a second ballot. We decided, 69 votes versus 23, to relocate and build a new church. Countless meetings followed. I will never forget the wonderful working relationship within the building committee. The sod-turning ceremony was held on July 31, 1961. We celebrated the dedication of the new Eden Mennonite Church on April 29, 1962.

Approximately two weeks before that joyous occasion, Brother H.H. Neufeld handed me his letter of resignation. I read the letter, then put it into my pocket and said: "Dear Brother Neufeld, this letter will stay in my pocket until the dedication of the church is history. Then I will present it to church council." Even though I was chairman of church council and the congregation, I was given no assignment in the dedication ceremonies.

As promised I presented H.H. Neufeld's written resignation at the first council meeting after the dedication. It was accepted with regret. The same happened at the subsequent congregational meeting. A few weeks later the deacons came to our farm to see me. I found it hard to believe that Brother Neufeld had been surprised that his resignation had been accepted without further discussion. I told those two wonderful brethren that I as chairman clearly rejected the idea of reopening the issue with either the council or the congregation. During H.H. Neufeld's last sermon at the Eden Church, the church council received a severe lecture. That was one of the most unpleasant experiences in all my church activities, even though since then I have had differences of opinion with leaders in church agencies.

We began our search for a new leading minister. Eden had several short-term pastors who succeeded H.H. Neufeld. First was Valentine Nickel, a wonderful dedicated senior pastor who died of cancer after a few years. Then from 1965-69 we had some marvellous years with Henry and Grace Wiens. But Grace wanted to go back to Saskatchewan so they did not stay long. For a short time Dietrich (Dick) Rempel became our interim pastor until we found George Groening. He had served several terms at Bethel Mennonite Church in Winnipeg and one at Foothills Mennonite Church in Calgary.

Our friendship with George and Nettie Groening went back to when I served on the Missions Committee of the B.C. Conference. I took issue with the Canadian Conference action to start a third Mennonite church in Chilliwack without consulting churches in the area. Groening was the Canadian Missions Committee representative at the February 1964 sessions of the B.C. Conference where I expressed my dismay. In March 1964 I received a letter from George:

> Siegfried, I would like to say that I appreciated your honesty and your boldness in opposing a thing that you felt was not right. I personally deeply respected you for it. May I say that I always respect a man for standing true to his convictions, even though I may not always agree with him.

In January 1971 Nettie and George came to B.C. to discuss with Eden members the possibility of George becoming our pastor. They had come by train and when we took them to the station in Agassiz, Nettie asked, with tears in her eyes, "Do you think we should try again to serve a church after our Calgary experience?" Things had not gone well for them there. We encouraged them strongly to come to Chilliwack.

George Groening served our church for 13 years until 1984. That was the time when our church experienced harmonious, clear leadership and the strongest growth in its history. In his last year, problems developed because some younger church members thought that pastors, like teachers, should retire at age 65. I am sure some middle-aged members also felt the same way, especially since the youth worker took the opportunity to work against George in a very unpleasant way. I was aware how that group felt so I told George what was happening. I suggested that he resign instead of waiting to be voted out. He did, but it was a very painful experience for both him and Nettie.

Church was very central in the life of our family. The boys all participated in the youth choir when they were at home. At that time this choir was the circle where youth who were interested in being active in church life took part. The boys were also all baptized on confession of their faith at the Eden Church. I continued as teacher in the German adult class from 1958 until the present (1994). In 1972 I was asked to assist in the German preaching. I was very aware that, at the time, this was an unusual request of someone who was not ordained.

40. Back to Family Farming

Our six-and-a-half years of partnership farming in Agassiz had ended on October 1, 1958, when Walter and Elfriede moved to their own farm. It had not always been easy but generally it had been a harmonious time. We continued our close contact with Walter and kept the silage machinery together. One of our major concerns was to increase the number of milk cows and to add to our milk quota. Walter and I maintained a healthy competition in the dairy herd aspect of our operations.

For the next ten years we farmed as Erna & Siegfried Bartel. The installation of a modern milking parlour made dairying much easier.

Our six sons in the mid-1970s (from tallest at right): Reinhard, Alex, Christoph, Dietrich, Gerd and Martin.

We also built the large loafing barn with cousins Ernst Bartel acting as architect and Hans-Peter Bartel as the main builder.

In the beginning of the 1960s we had very good farm workers. By the later '60s our sons had taken on more responsibility. Reinhard, who graduated from the agriculture program at Chilliwack Senior High School, stayed home for two years to farm with me. He was followed by Christoph. Then on June 30, 1968, my dream was fulfilled. Christoph joined us as shareholder in Birchlane Farms Ltd.

At the entrance to my parents farm in West Prussia had been a 200-metre-long lane with large, beautiful birch trees. To nurture our memories of the old country, we had planted a row of birches on either side of the lane leading to our farm in Agassiz. Birchlane Farms seemed like a fitting name for our newly established company. The estimated value of the whole operation was $198,751. The mortgage from the Farm Credit Corporation was $38,018.03; the second mortgage with *Auslandsiedlung* was $6,230.57. The bank loan was $9,461.81, leaving a cash value of the operation at $145,040.59.

When Christoph joined the farm we discontinued raising raspberries and increased the cattle herd again. After only four years on the farm, he said to me one day: "Papi, I now know that I will not be milking cows all my life."

Christoph, who had married Lillian Enns in February 1969, left the farm in 1972. We had worked together harmoniously. When he moved away, I wiped tears from my eyes. For the time being the dream of farming with one of our sons came to an end. The separation was hard for both Christoph and me.

From 1972 to 1976 Ernusch and I kept the Birchlane Farm operation going. We again had to rely on hired help, especially since I had taken on several public positions which demanded much of my time. We were fortunate to find an excellent man, John Wynia, with whom we enjoyed working together. When I was out of the province Ernusch felt quite secure with him at home.

Along with developments in our farming situation also came changes in our family life. We were thankful for our six wonderful sons. Naturally, it was up to them to find their life partners, thereby *choosing our daughters*. Ernusch had often wondered out loud how she would handle the situation when girls would become part of the family. I assured her that I would joyfully assist her. Three years after Ernusch and I celebrated our 25th wedding anniversary, when Martin was only ten years old, the first daughter joined the family. Gerd and Regina's wedding took place in 1967.

Our boys had arrived at about two or three year intervals. The interludes between their weddings were approximately the same. By 1979 all six sons were married. Our sons differ one from the other, but our daughters-in-law even more. As we love and appreciate our sons, so we enjoy and love their life partners.

Ernusch has often said, "I have not borne and raised girls and have no way of comparing daughters and daughters-in law. Therefore, to me they are all daughters."

It was in summer 1969 that Ernusch and I went on a trip to Europe. Reinhard was working with MCC in France (later Switzerland). We took the train to New York and from there sailed to Europe on the new Queen Elizabeth II. We met Reinhard in Le Havre. It was not easy for Ernusch to go on that trip. Martin was only 12 years old and we left him with his brothers. The picture of Martin waving and running beside the train when it pulled out of the station in Agassiz remained with Ernusch during the entire trip. Gerd and Regina spent their holidays at our farm house and cared for the brothers at home. Christoph and Lillian, the farm couple, lived in the small house that we had moved there from a near-by farm.

In 1976, when we realized that Martin at age 19 was interested in farming, we took him into the Company as shareholder. The full value of the Birchlane Farms' shares was estimated at $276,000. Martin bought one-third for $92,000 in terms payable over 17 years.

Our retirement home on the "mountain" on Tuyttens Road near Agassiz

One day in spring of 1978 I was driving along Tuyttens Road with John Wynia. I noticed a "For Sale" sign on the mountain which belonged to Mr. Caignon on the farm adjacent to ours. The sign had actually been placed on a small part of our property which was cut off when I gave the Municipality of Kent permission to build a shortcut on Tuyttens Road. I went to Funk Agencies, our local real estate agent, to ask them to move the sign. While I was in the office someone phoned and asked the agent for the price of the mountain. When I heard $58,000, I went home to talk to Ernusch about buying it. I returned to the office the same day but it was already closed. In the evening I talked to Gerd who suggested that I should offer $50,000 for the property. At 9:00 a.m. sharp next morning I was at the office with that offer. The bank next door had no objection to lending me the cash. By that evening the deal was signed.

At that time, Martin was engaged to Wanda and we were planning to move off the farm. In fall 1978 we started building our retirement home on the south tip of that newly acquired mountain property. The house was ready at Easter in 1979, a few weeks before Martin and Wanda's wedding. The building costs were $77,000, including floors and drapes. Not included in the price were wages for Hans-Peter Bartel who helped build the house and gave valuable advice.

Moving off the farm was an emotional experience, even though our youngest son and his wife were taking over the operation. It was there we had raised our family and where we had enjoyed the longest period of our pilgrimage together. For over 20 years I had been the farm manager. The boys and highly qualified farm workers had participated in the operation but I had always been the final decision-maker. That changed when we moved off the farm. A new era was about to begin. A different approach to management was a natural development, but not easy to accept.

V

Entering the Public Arena

After 14 years on the school board, I had become fairly fluent in the English language, I had learned how to conduct meetings, and had come to realize the limitations of public office. But I had also been made aware of the tremendous responsibilities of decision making.

41. An Immigrant on the School Board

During the summer of 1960 I received a visit from the mayor of Agassiz, Jim Fraser, a highly respected senior leader in the community. He suggested that I should run for the position of trustee on the school board. By that time we had five boys in school. We had shown interest in school affairs, including participation in the Parent-Teacher Association. But our ability to handle the English language was still limited. Even when Fraser suggested that I *run* for one of the positions on the school board, I did not fully understand what he meant. For me the word run had only one meaning as in a 100-metre dash. I was too ashamed to let him know my problem, so after he left I talked to our friend Bob Marriot, the milk tester, and asked for an explanation. Bob smiled and explained.

We thought about the benefits of having an influence on school affairs, especially since all of our boys were in the public school system. I decided to file papers for the election. It came as a great surprise to me when I won. I had been up against Mrs. Gairns, a long-time board member and respected member in the community. She was also the local reporter for the *Agassiz-Harrison Advance*. Her disappointment influenced the press coverage I received in the local paper for years to come. When I decided to run I didn't have the slightest idea what all the implications would be.

As a new board member, I spent the first two years mainly learning, not only the rules and the proceedings but also the language. During our first nine years in Canada, our English vocabulary focused primarily on the farming scene and on church life, not on the educational field. In the school board discussions I prepared my questions before I spoke.

Some time in my second or third year I learned a valuable lesson. During a ball game at the school, some students displayed unacceptable behaviour. Not giving sufficient recognition to the fact that the teachers were in charge of the event, I made some comments about the situation. At the next board meeting the spokesperson for the teachers complained to the board on behalf of the teachers. The day after the meeting Mrs. Pretty, the chairperson, phoned me and encouraged me not to be down on myself and not to be silent when

I was not in agreement with the position of others. I was tremendously thankful for her encouragement. I had seriously considered discontinuing my membership on the board.

Toward the end of 1965, Mr. Alexander, the superintendent of the school district, approached me, apparently on behalf of other board members, and asked me to take on responsibilities as chairperson of the Board of School Trustees for the coming year. I was astonished at his request. I replied that my less-than-perfect English was barely sufficient to contribute to the board's discussion, and that I would not feel comfortable chairing the meetings.

I remember his reply very distinctly, "Siegfried, we know you make mistakes when you speak English, but we always know exactly what you mean."

I was approached to take the chair because decision-making under Mrs. Pretty's direction was sometimes a slow process. I held that wonderful person in high regard, but sometimes she dragged out the meetings until midnight when we thought we could have been finished by 10:00 p.m. I accepted the chair and served in that position for nine years.

During my years on the school board I had excellent relationships with my fellow board members, with the staff at the board office and, most of the time, with the teachers. It was a challenge for an immigrant, only recently arrived in Canada, with limited knowledge of the English language and clearly identified as a German to hold such a prominent position.

One thing I learned very explicitly was that the individual board member had little impact on school affairs, but the entire board could have far-reaching influence. I recall several issues on which I had an effect on the board as a whole. In 1965 I was able to convince the board of the urgent need for a kindergarten. We became the first school district in the Fraser Valley to introduce such a program. At the same time we introduced swimming instruction in Grade 5, with the goal that eventually every Agassiz student would learn to swim.

In 1968 we accepted a proposal from the Department of Indian Affairs that all high school students from the Seabird Island and Chehalis reserves be integrated. That action was followed by joint meetings of our board with the education committees from the two reserves. Later on we appointed someone from the native community as a member on the Agassiz-Harrison School Board. That was the best time ever for cooperation in the education field with the native community in our area. In 1970 we introduced the position of a coordinator for Indian students. For a number of years there were better relations between the board and native people, but it was not easy to fill the position with someone who was able to cooperate with the school and actually be helpful to native students.

The situation is always difficult when highly respected leaders get old and are no longer capable of working in positions which they filled successfully for many years. We had such an experience with Mr. Duncan, principal of the Agassiz High School. Mr. Moulds was a capable vice-principal and the two got along very well. In 1968, my third year as chairperson, it became my responsibility to talk to Mr. Duncan and try to convince him to resign as principal and accept the vice-principal role for the rest of his teaching career. Who was I to tell someone that he was no longer doing his job? I received Mr. Duncan's full cooperation and he graciously moved to the vice-principal position.

My personal relationship with Mr. Duncan went through several stages. One experience came long before I became a member on the school board. When our son Reinhard was not promoted from Grade 2 to Grade 3 I had a discussion with him. The action was clearly based only on the fact that Reinhard did not know the English language well enough. Duncan criticized us as parents for not speaking English with the boys at home. I explained to him that the boys would not be able to learn English from us because we did not know the language well enough to be of any help to them.

Other students stated it plainly, "We know why Reinhard was not promoted. He is German." When I became chairperson of the board I thought about that incident many times. However, I did not allow my personal agenda to intrude in our relationship.

We were fortunate in later years to have two outstanding principals, Mr. Moulds in the high school and Mr. Zebroff in the elementary school. Illegal drug use was becoming more common among the young people in those years, and Agassiz was no exception. We had a policy of dismissing students when they were caught with drugs, no exceptions allowed, regardless of whether it was the daughter of a board member, the son of a senior teacher or the daughter of our best neighbour and friend. Exercising that discipline was not an easy task, especially in a small community.

Moral standards were very important, but the interpretation could become difficult if there was no way of stating the facts publicly when disagreements arose. That happened in June 1972 when the mother of a Grade 12 student came to the board with her daughter's diary.

In it she had written in detail about her relationship to a certain teacher who had been giving her rides home from school.

Since the school was responsible to ensure that bus students actually went home by bus and not in a teacher's car, we sought counsel from the board's lawyer. Since that teacher was in his probationary year, the board decided not to keep him on staff. He was well liked in the community and by the staff, and an uproar ensued. Ernusch and I were visiting with relatives in Calgary when the issue became public. We were called home by phone. The president of the local teacher's association wrote a critical letter to the board, stating that "the board finds itself isolated" on this issue. Some even suggested holding demonstrations on our farm.

In a letter to the editor of the *Agassiz-Harrison Advance*, Gerry Freeman wrote:

> In talking with a member of the local school board, I was told that Perry Long was a talented teacher. The reason for termination of his employment was because of his differences with administration, that means the principal, Mr. Gerry Moulds, and the superintendent, Mr. Alexander. In other words: to hell with whether or not he is a good teacher and an asset to the school. There is a difference of opinion and he must go. . . .
>
> There are many questions that deserve an answer in this whole deal. Most of all I feel the students of Mr. Long deserve the answers. If they don't get them, I sincerely feel they should get their parents and attend the next school board meeting on Wednesday, June 21.

The June 21 meeting was dramatic. A large delegation brought a petition signed by many people. The *Agassiz Advance* reported:

> The other side of this large gathering was referred to as a "pressure group" by Chairman Bartel. This group included many interested parents, citizens, a teacher from Chilliwack, a local school teacher, the mayor of Harrison and students. Chairman Bartel stated at the beginning that the board would listen to this group but would not argue any point. He also stated that the board would not be pressured by this group.

Many came to Mr. Long's defense. Students and other teachers lauded Mr. Long as an "outstanding teacher." The mayor and president of the Teachers Society said that the board "should take a real sound second look at their decision." But we remained firm in our decision not to keep Mr. Long on permanent staff.

The opposite reaction developed when the daughter of a prominent family had decided one night to leave her room via a window
and ladder to have a rendezvous with a certain teacher on the shores
of Harrison Lake. The board was approached by the mother of that
young lady. A member of the clergy asked us to fire the teacher from
the Agassiz High School. There weren't adequate grounds for doing
so, but the rumour spread that the board was endorsing low moral
standards. Those concerns came to a climax with the approval of a
statement by the school board at its March 1974 meeting.

The statement confirmed that "trends toward permissiveness and
lack of structure in education are not in the best interests of the
pupils." It put the onus on the board "to hire teachers for our district
who favour discipline and the emphasis of a solid ground in the
fundamental skills." Furthermore, parents and teachers alike were
challenged to "make a positive contribution toward a disciplined
school situation . . . The board must comply with the requirements
of the School Act, that 'the highest morality shall be inculcated.'"

In its March 21, 1974, issue, the *Advance* reported:

> There were several split votes on amendments which had to be
> decided by Chairman Siegfried Bartel, and he also cast the deciding
> vote for acceptance of the statement. . . . Mr. Bartel's vote also
> decided that the statement would not become part of the board's
> book of policies.

The never-ending challenge of how to keep the lines of communication open between the board and the general public was a special
concern of mine. Dr. Emil and Mrs. Mary Grieshabber sent me a leter
of encouragement after that meeting:

> [We] want to tell you that you did a fine job of chairing the meeting
> at the school last night. It is a difficult thing to get people started in
> airing their opinions and once started, to keep them on the track
> toward useful conclusions. You did just that last night, and in a way
> that had great charm. Everyone who spoke, I'm sure, felt he had a
> fair hearing, and most important, that what he or she had to say was
> listened to.
> The young people of the school have great admiration for the
> even-handed way you manage contacts with them.

For the 1972-73 school year I was elected as chairperson of the
Fraser Valley Branch of School Trustees. In those years the trustees

received an annual honorarium of $1,300; the following year that was raised to $1,861. During the time I held that office I travelled to Quebec City for the convention of Canadian School Trustees to represent our branch. That gave me an opportunity to visit the harbour in Quebec City where our family entered Canada on May 7, 1951.

At the first meeting of the Board of School Trustees in 1974 I had announced that I would not seek re-election after my term expired at the end of the year. The December 9, 1974, minutes of the Board, my last meeting as a member, mention that I spoke briefly:

> He had especially enjoyed working for the Indian children and stated the Agassiz-Harrison School District was one of the first districts to have an Indian Home and School Co-ordinator and also one of the first districts to have a Native Indian School Trustee. Mr. Bartel said that there will be times when the public may be misled by pressure groups and will not be in support of your decisions and stated that his faith and his beliefs had guided him to act responsibly and suggested that in a similar manner trustees can act responsibly for the children of the district and also the community.

After 14 years on the Board of School Trustees in Agassiz I had become fairly fluent in the English language, I had learned how to conduct meetings and had come to realize the limitations of public office. But I had also been made aware of the tremendous responsibilities of decision making.

42. Advocate for the Doukhobors

In 1966, the first year I was chairman of the school board, I received a telephone call from Dr. Kennedy, Deputy Attorney General of British Columbia. He had received reports that I had made personal contact with the Sons of Freedom Doukhobor group which had camped outside the gates of the Agassiz Federal Prison Institution for a number of years. Dr. Kennedy wondered if I would be willing to become more involved in helping the government "deal with" the Doukhobors.

My experiences with the Doukhobors went back several months when we had torn down two buildings on our farm. They were willing to do the job, provided we would keep only the heavy lumber and they could take the rest. At the time we were also constructing two liquid manure tanks, putting a roof on our old hip-roof barn and building an open-area loafing barn. We did all that work primarily with the help of Doukhobor carpenters and labourers.

Ever since the Doukhobors had emigrated to Canada in 1899, they had resisted the principle of individual land ownership and the practice of registering births, deaths and marriages. In their refusal to accept the laws of Canada on those issues, they sometimes resorted to demonstrations, occasionally even removing their clothing for extra emphasis. After they moved to British Columbia, the question of their children's attendance at public schools became the focal point of resistance to governmental authority.

When an attempt to establish their own school system failed, their leader, Peter P. Virigin, "made a general commitment on behalf of all Doukhobors to support the public schools" (William Janzen, *Limits on Liberty*, 9-10). However, some Doukhobor opposition to public schools remained. That faction became known as the Sons of Freedom Doukhobors. They responded to the situation by using nudity and burning down their houses to indicate resistance.

In 1955, 104 children were forcibly removed from their parents and taken to a school surrounded by barbed wire in New Denver. A total of 170 children passed through that institution in its six-year history.

There were many nude demonstrations and burnings. The court proceedings were sometimes hampered by the willingness of individuals "to suffer" with those who were imprisoned. Some even voluntarily pleaded guilty for acts in which they had not participated.

Throughout the struggle with the Doukhobor community there always were educators, politicians and other individuals who tried to relate to them and influence them. The government did little to come to terms with them peacefully.

In 1962 the Federal Government built a special prison camp in Agassiz for the Sons of Freedom Doukhobors. That resulted in a decision by the prisoners' relatives to make the trek from their homes in the Kootenay Valley to Agassiz. First, the Freedomites marched to Vancouver. Then, in July 1963, approximately 500 of them set up camps at the gates of the Federal prison in Agassiz where some of the men were being held. The *Advance* reported that in August there were 68 tents in the gravel pit and 79 Doukhobor children were attending Agassiz schools.

In principle, the Doukhobors are a peace-loving people. They were simply standing up for what they believed were their rights. But they

The Doukhobor "village" set up in July 1963 outside the gates of the Federal prison in Agassiz.

were not treated very well by the justice system. One example of the mistreatment of Doukhobors was the withholding of their welfare payments. The *Agassiz Advance* advocated a more humane position in an editorial on September 19, 1963:

> When the Freedomites lived in the Kootenays, they received provincial welfare payments. When they camped at Hope they didn't. When they moved to Vancouver they got the money again. Now that they are in Agassiz they don't. There appears to be a policy, but a rather odd one. . . .
>
> When there is no attempt to exert either authority or pressure, when police stand by while sect members break the law, when government buses are chartered to provide transportation, when provincial health authorities assist in making the camp safely inhabitable—where on earth is the sense of trying to exert pressure through withholding welfare? We hold no brief for the Freedomites, but there are times when their rejection of Canadian authority is not hard to understand.

Fuel was added to the fire of the radical elements within the Doukhobor group in 1964 when Simma Holt's book, *Terror in the Name of God*, was published. The campers believed that all of society looked at their problems the way Simma Holt did. However, an editorial in the November 26, 1964, *Agassiz Advance* said otherwise.

Mrs. Holt's theme is an excellent one—arguing the need to break the chain by which the children in each successive generation are warped to serve twisted doctrines for the profit of a few unscrupulous leaders. Her "solution" to the problem, however, seems to us a couple of years out of date, if society would ever have stood for it at all.

Briefly, she would take the children away from the parents. . . . all that needed doing along that line was done when the children were rounded up and held at the New Denver school. Unable to obtain their release any other way, the parents were forced to permit school attendance in order to get their children back. That decision seems to have been taken once and for all.

The years since then . . . the children are in school, in most cases as a small minority among non-Doukhobor pupils. Even some of the adults, most of whom must of necessity be followers, not leaders, are plainly taking a new look at the situation. And there hasn't been any destructive demonstration worth mentioning since 1962. If things carry on in like manner for another half dozen years, there is good reason to hope that the problem will be gone. In other words, we think "the solution" is already in operation.

That was the situation when I received the call from Dr. Kennedy, asking me if I would take an assignment to relate more personally to the Freedomites in the Agassiz camp. I accepted his invitation, but on the condition that the RCMP's D-Squad and its Russian-speaking officers would be withdrawn from regularly patrolling the camp (the public interpreted the "D" to stand for Doukhobor, but the RCMP explained that it stood for "Depredation").

At that time the decision-making role within the Sons of Freedom Doukhobors was entirely in the hands of women. That trend had developed when the majority of men were imprisoned and Fanny Storgoff had taken on the leadership role. After her death in September 1964 no one stepped forward as leader and consequently a group of women served as spokespersons and decision-makers.

The Freedomites had just started the struggle to get their spiritual leader, Stefan Sorokin, back to Canada from Uruguay. On December 12, 1968, the *Agassiz Advance* reported that "about forty students from the Freedomite camp have been kept out of Agassiz schools by their parents for the past two weeks, apparently in protest over refusal of Immigration authorities to let their spiritual leader, Stefan Sorokin, return to Canada for a visit."

That's where I as chairperson of the public school board came into the picture. I accepted the challenge wholeheartedly by meeting the female leadership group. At the beginning of the dialogue with the Freedomite women, I stated that I was coming to them as chairman of the local school board, as a local farmer who had been acquainted with many of them, and as a dedicated Christian who was willing to help them in our common goal of achieving peace.

I did that, knowing with absolute certainty that I was dealing with people who had turned to fanaticism because of irresponsible leaders and because of the treatment they had received from authorities. The latter had made no efforts to understand either them or the principles and beliefs they held dear.

The women repeated that their main concern was to get an entrance visa for Mr. Sorokin. I knew there was one person I could count on for help: Magistrate William Evans, a Juvenile and Family Court judge in the counties of Yale and Kootenay. Even when he, in his position as judge, was sentencing the Sons of Freedom to prison terms, he always managed to show a personal side in his relationship to these people.

On December 10, 1968, he had written a letter to Jerry Pringle, Member of Parliament for Fraser Valley East, in which he said:

> As I have been involved in Doukhobor affairs since I was appointed to the Bench about 20 years ago, I met Mr. S.S. Sorokin many times at my home and office to discuss matters concerning his followers. I received the last letter from him on the 27th of November last, in which he stated that he was unable to get a visa, that he wanted to visit Canada to see those of his followers and his son Billy. I would say that I know him better than any other non-Doukhobor. I always found him to be a gentleman and there is not the slightest doubt that he has been a great asset to me in dealing with the Sons of Freedom.
>
> You will recall that in 1959 I gave an order releasing the Doukhobor children from the New Denver Dormitory School, where they were being kept as wards of the Supt. of Child Welfare for non-school attendance. At that time the parents promised me they would send their children to public school if returned to them. They kept their promise and the children have an excellent attendance record, until this recent occurrence. Just prior to releasing the children the mothers refused to sign an undertaking, and only did so after I had wired Mr. Sorokin who was then in Uruguay, to advise them, which he did. One delegation of mothers last week reminded me that the only reason they now send the children to public school was because Sorokin told them he would not have anything further to do with them if they did not obey the law. . . .
>
> For years now the Sons of Freedom, or Reformed Doukhobors, have been law abiding and we have not had the slightest trouble here.

... I know of no reason why Mr. Sorokin should be denied a visa. He has, while in British Columbia, always obeyed the law. . . . In any case he is the Spiritual Leader of the Sons of Freedom. If they wish him to return, I see no reason why he should not. I recommend that he be given a visa for a three month visit if that is what he wants.

By December 18, Dr. Kennedy had recognized my involvement and positive influence in getting the Sons of Freedom children back to school. In a letter he said:

If the newspaper reports are accurate, you have been very successful in your meetings with the Freedomite parents. I hope you finally managed to talk to the parents and not just the grandparents.

This letter is primarily to thank you for your efforts in getting the children back to school pending clarification of the parents' and grandparents' problem with Ottawa which really has nothing to do with the children. By way of information to you, I have forwarded to the Department of Immigration at Ottawa the original appeal written by the mothers at Agassiz and forwarded to Magistrate Evans at Nelson. . . .

However, the issue of getting permission for Sorokin to come to Canada was by no means settled. For January 7, 1969, I had arranged a meeting between Jerry Pringle and the women leadership of the camp. He had promised "to bring as much information as possible from the Minister of Immigration, and to take any submissions from them to Ottawa for direct consultation with the Minister."

When we arrived, approximately 30 to 40 women were assembled in their community hall to present their concerns to Mr. Pringle. As they usually did, the spokesperson presented the group's concerns in the Russian language, and one of the younger women translated into English. Of course, their main concern was to get an entrance visa for Mr. Sorokin. Mr. Pringle promised that he would do all he could, but the decision was up to the Ministry of Manpower and Immigration. That was not good enough for them and they became quite excited. I informed Mr. Pringle that we should leave the assembly hall, but Mr. Pringle continued to explain details of the procedure.

I started to walk out. Within a few seconds all the women had dropped their clothes and were in the nude, lamenting in the Russian language. Mr. Pringle then realized that was not a conducive atmosphere for further dialogue, so he left the room as well, trying not to step on the clothes lying on the floor.

In the evening some men came to see me and apologized for the behaviour of the women. At a meeting next morning with the leaders of the group, I asked them the reason for their behaviour.

They said, "In our struggle over so many years that action became our sign of showing our helplessness toward authority."

Finally, in April 1969, Pringle wrote to the "Doukhobor Mothers at Agassiz:"

> I am writing to advise that the Immigration Department has completed the processing of Mr. Stefan S. Sorokin's application for a visa. I am happy to advise that it has been granted and I know of no obstacle to prevent his entry into Canada.

Some time later Mr. Sorokin arrived in Canada. He did not stay in Agassiz long, but before he moved to the Kootenay Valley he visited us on our farm. We had coffee together and talked about many issues. He spoke no English but could speak some German. Someone translated his Russian comments into English and mine into Russian.

A group of Doukhobors moved back to the Kootenay Valley with Mr. Sorokin, and the question was raised: How long will the rest of the group stay at the roadside camp in Agassiz? In 1970, John Green, editor of *The Advance*, reported:

> The last of the Freedomite prisoners is gone from Mountain Prison, and with him the last flimsy excuse for the existence of the Freedomite camp outside the fence. . . . That the camp ever existed in the first place reflects the inability of the senior governments to carry out their plain duty, and to enforce their own laws. The basic approach has been to ignore the whole thing and hope that no more serious trouble would develop, and that eventually the problem would go away. The first hope has been realized, but not the second. . . . There is no need to cause hardship, and no need for haste, but the need to remove the camp should be publicly recognized as of now, and the steps to bring that about should be begun.

During 1971 the camp was calm, and the situation with the campers' children at school was normal. Nevertheless, on May 29 of that year the *Agassiz Advance* reported that 29 children from the camp were absent from school protesting court proceedings connected to some cases of arson in the Kootenay Valley. More and more members of the group moved back to the area where the majority of them resided.

*John Dunshan, a Doukhobor
leader and our friend.*

A rumour circulated in Agassiz that a group of hippies was planning to move into the empty space at the camp. Some local people wanted to prevent that from happening and threatened to burn down the camps.

One evening several Freedomite families—among them John Dunshan, one of their leaders and my friend—came to our farm and asked for permission to stay at our house for the night. They were frightened by the threats being directed at the camp. Ernusch and I were on a trip to northern B.C. at the time. But our family members distinctly remember John Dunshan praying in the Russian language as they stood around the table at the evening meal and breakfast the following morning with our Doukhobor friends.

The threats became reality. When the camp burned down, one chapter came to an end. Even after that, some extremists within that group did not cooperate despite their difficult experiences in Agassiz. A few incidents of arson and nude demonstrations took place, but for the majority there finally was peace. An accord had been achieved through different means than *authoritarian violence*.

The many hours I had spent with that group—people who deep down were honest, hard-working individuals, people who had been misled by their leaders to unacceptable acts—were not spent in vain. The long chain of violence had come to an end. More valuable to me than the Deputy Attorney General's acknowledgement of my efforts was the lasting friendship with many individuals of the Sons of Freedom Doukhobors who are now living peacefully within society.

43. Beginning Inter-Mennonite Involvements

In 1966, the year I became chairman of the Agassiz-Harrison School Board, I also joined the board of the Mennonite Benevolent Society. That gave me my first taste of inter-Mennonite work. The Benevolent Society was founded by members of the Conference of Mennonites in British Columbia. Its goal from the time it was formed in 1952 was to work together with the Mennonite Brethren churches in B.C. for the benefit of all seniors in the Fraser Valley. However, when the Mennonite Brethren established Tabor Home several years later, very few of them continued as board members on the Mennonite Benevolent Society.

That was a special phase in my church involvements because I could work side by side on the board with Onkel Rempel, our senior family friend, our Canadian guide and our farm sponsor. Onkel Rempel served on the board from 1965 to 1969, I from 1966 to 1971. It also gave me an opportunity to work with members of the Eden Mennonite Church who played an important role in the Mennonite Benevolent Society.

Little did I know at the time that that was only the beginning of many years of working with people from many different Mennonite denominations. It was a valuable time of learning and becoming acquainted with inter-Mennonite relations.

In 1970 I joined the executive of Mennonite Central Committee in B.C. When I accepted the position of chairman of that board in 1972, I decided not to let my name stand for re-election on the Board of the Mennonite Benevolent Society.

44. First Foray into MCC Work

A telephone call one day in late summer of 1970 ushered me into two decades of memorable experiences in church-related work. Jake Tilitzky, moderator of the Conference of Mennonites in B.C., asked if I would let my name stand as representative of that Conference on the executive of Mennonite Central Committee (MCC) in B.C. He assured me that the executive had only four regular meetings a year.

I agreed, especially since I did not feel needed as an active participant in my home congregation, yet wanted some involvement in church life. On October 31, 1970, at the annual delegate meeting of MCC B.C. held at Eden Church, I was elected to the board.

Mennonite Central Committee was *the* Mennonite organization which we had always held in highest regard. We were familiar with it since childhood days in the 1920s when the stream of refugees came from Russia. Our Mennonite churches in Germany worked in partnership with MCC to help those refugees on their journey to North and South America. After the Second World War, when we ourselves were displaced persons from our homeland, Prussia, and became refugees in West Germany, the name MCC always brought a glimmer of hope when we thought about our personal future. C.F. Klassen and the organization he represented became an important part of discussions, especially when we decided to emigrate to Canada. Now, approximately 20 years later, I had the opportunity to be part of that organization.

As a newly elected member on the executive of MCC B.C., I was impressed with the harmonious working relationship between representatives from the Conference of Mennonite in B.C. and the provincial Mennonite Brethren Conference. Earlier, as a delegate to the MCC B.C. annual meetings, I had been critical that board members received an honorarium, albeit very small, for every meeting they attended. At my first executive meeting I made the motion to do away with that policy. The motion was passed without discussion. That opened the way for me to be much more aggressive in fundraising for MCC.

Before long, my involvement with MCC increased considerably. When George Thielmann resigned as chairperson on November 4, 1971, I was elected to replace him. The minutes of that meeting read: "Mr. Bartel takes over the chairmanship at this time and requests the patience, understanding and cooperation of the committee members, and with God's help he is willing to fulfil this post to the furtherance of God's Kingdom." Accepting the chairmanship of a provincial MCC board automatically included being the representative on the board of MCC Canada and MCC (binational).

In 1971 during my first full year on the board, the B.C. agenda had required some very important decisions. The need arose to change to monthly meetings. My somewhat more aggressive approach to decision making seemed appropriate for three important decisions which had to be made during my first years as chairman.

First, we established the position of a full-time executive secretary for MCC B.C. With that move came the acceptance of full responsibility for the Western Canadian clothing depot in Yarrow. Until then the depot had been operated by MCC Canada from the Winnipeg office. The selection of a suitable person for the executive secretary position was not easy. By August 23, 1971, we had received three applicants. None seemed quite appropriate. I believed that we should have a returned MCC worker who could interpret the overseas program effectively to the constituency.

We contacted the office in Akron for suggestions. They informed us that Vernon Reimer would be returning to North America from India where he had served for ten years as country director. Their recommendation was not entirely favourable. I was told that Vernon made decisions very independently and that the Akron office had some difficulties working with him. I recall saying that I would have no problems in that regard.

The executive minutes of November 4, 1971 recorded: "After considering the applications and the priorities, the Board favoured the appointment of Brother Vernon Reimer." Brother Vernon served our constituency for three years. He was outstanding in organizing the newly established office and in serving the churches as ambassador of MCC. In his report to the 1975 annual meeting he stated:

> In closing I wish to make special mention of the dedicated and concerned leadership your Executive Committee under the chairmanship of Siegfried Bartel has provided. How often they grappled with difficult issues, realizing that we are not always agreed but wanting to make that decision that would be most pleasing to God and would have the general support of you as members. As returned overseas workers, we have felt so comfortable to find such dedicated and able people guiding and supporting this phase of the churches' program.

The second important issue with which the executive dealt during my first year as chairman was the question of relocating the MCC B.C. office and warehouse from Yarrow to Clearbrook. At a special delegate meeting on April 26, 1971, the executive was given the go-ahead to "come up with a definite proposal" by the fall meeting. In October we were authorized "to initiate the purchase of suitable property for the purpose of relocating the MCC B.C. warehouse and offices to a more central location." It took until the December 12, 1973, meeting before we considered specific properties. We agreed on a one-acre lot on Marshall Road that had been offered free of cost by Albert Toews if MCC would build there. That plan materialized and the building was dedicated in May 1975. Jake Siemens, who acted as representative of the MCC board and as builder, deserved a lot of credit in that project. His dedicated and unselfish service made it possible to keep down the cost of the facilities.

The third important issue facing the executive at that time was whether a project for the mentally handicapped people should be included in MCC B.C.'s program. We were first approached by David A. Friesen of the Samaritan Society for Comfort and Cheer in May 1972 whether we would sponsor or take over a project of that nature. At the fall meeting we agreed to ask the Society for "a more thorough project proposal before we could make any further decisions." A year later the delegates approved the executive recommendation that "MCC B.C. take over the Samaritan Society's entire project in the present state of establishing a home for the physically and mentally disabled."

During my years as chairperson of MCC B.C. that program grew enormously. It included a number of residential homes—The Cedars in Rosedale and Twin Firs in Huntington near Abbotsford—as well as a camping program for the mentally handicapped and a community living program. As reported in a book telling the story of MCC B.C.,

Sodturning in 1974 for the new MCC B.C. building on Marshall Road in Clearbrook which was dedicated in May 1975.

In November 1988 the annual revenue was in excess of $1.2 million: $880,000 from government contracts, $150,000 from MCC (B.C.) and other donations, and the remainder from the sale of produce at Twin Firs [a home for mentally handicapped adults] and labour contracts (i.e., janitorial). This money was spent on paying 40 full-time and five part-time staff persons, giving residential care to 51 persons and day-care programs to another 25 (Helen Grace Lescheid, ed., *Footprints of Compassion*, 55).

The project grew so much that, at the 1991 annual meeting, the executive presented a proposal to allow Supportive Care Services, as it came to be called, to have its own legal identity. No other provincial MCC had done anything comparable for our mentally handicapped.

I was asked often, "Are you not afraid that this program is growing too rapidly?"

My reply always was, "If the growth is needed to serve people, then I have no concern at all, as long as the administration is not growing faster than the program of service."

Another area in which MCC B.C. was launching out on a new venture in the early 1970s was the relief sale. On March 14, 1970, the B.C. Auction Committee was elected by MCC representatives of all (Mennonite) B.C. churches. It was decided to have a committee of seven brothers. Their first report to the executive stated, in part:

It was soon evident that we would need some representation from our ladies and somewhat belated two of our very active ladies were elected into the same committee. We were told: there is no money for you to start a sale; you may start one now but you are on your own. We had a total of 26 meetings of prayer and business in less than six months. On September 12, 1970, we had the Auction Sale (the first one) with more than 6,000 people attending. The same netted MCC (B.C.) in excess of $21,000 in cash.

By the annual meeting on November 1, 1975, a motion was passed to hold the relief sales annually.

The growth of relief sale activities was overwhelming. I valued that program as special for a number of reasons: it raised money for MCC work worldwide; it was a great testimony to society about what could be done by the church on a volunteer basis; it was a great time to make friends; and it was a wonderful way to involve as organizers and volunteers hundreds of people who, generally speaking, were often less prominent in internal church life.

Presiding at an MCC B.C. executive meeting.

For a number of years, toward the end of my chairmanship on the MCC B.C. executive, members and senior staff visited every leading pastor of our constituency churches in Vancouver and the Fraser Valley. We went to encourage them to send their full slate of delegates (one delegate per 30 members) and to discuss and review MCC-related issues. It was sad that many pastors were so eager to emphasize the need for funds for their own local programs at the expense of paying less and less attention to the plight of the poor around the world. Very few pastors attended annual meetings and those who did spoke up very little.

Another area where we did not achieve success was in our attempt to get more young church members to our annual meetings. Historically, it was emigrants who experienced help from MCC. Therefore, the work in and with MCC was seen as belonging to the older generation. I pray that might change. Otherwise the future of MCC could be in jeopardy.

MCC B.C. was involved in many other projects than those mentioned above: thrift stores and the furniture store, the Golden Age Society, work with native people of our land in Port Hardy and the establishment of the MCC B.C. Housing Society. Those stories are all recorded in the book *Footprints of Compassion*.

On March 6, 1988, I concluded my service with MCC B.C. after 18 years. In my farewell address at the November 6, 1988, annual meeting, I presented a challenge to those present. I indicated that my vision for MCC B.C was two-pronged: that it increase the program of Supportive Care Services and that its work be extended to include the growing geriatric population.

My other concerns were more general. One was Jesus' teaching on dealing with the poor. To the gathered delegates I said:

> In general, we Evangelicals emphasize the main task of the church as bringing people to *know* Jesus Christ, to accept him as Lord and Saviour, but we are neglecting his teachings about our relationship to the poor. . . . In large segments in our churches, members are criticizing MCC for speaking out on issues related to the poor. . . . it is my prayer that the church, and MCC particularly, will not grow weary of calling on the governments if we feel that the concern for the poor is neglected. . . .

During my years with MCC I struggled to come to terms with my involvement as a soldier and officer in the war. At times feelings of guilt became overwhelming. Although I had not spoken publicly about my personal struggles, at this last meeting with MCC B.C. I challenged my fellow board members:

> One concern I have for MCC on all levels: that MCC should never grow weary in teaching, preaching and proclaiming Jesus' position on peace: "Pursue peace with all, and the sanctification without which no one will see the Lord" (Hebrews 12:14).

Leaving MCC B.C. (at back): Waldo Neufeld, executive secretary; (at right): David Giesbrecht, vice-chairman.

In our evangelical churches, and many Mennonite churches included, we have quickly accepted the "just war theory" and therefore we are quiet on the question of the arms race. . . .

We, the peace churches, have to speak out. . . . We, the followers of Jesus Christ, have to take our guidance, our directions, from God and God alone. We have to be careful about the propaganda of the state, regardless how coloured it may be presented. May the vision of MCC on proclaiming, teaching and *living* according to the example of Jesus Christ never get dim.

David Giesbrecht responded on behalf of MCC B.C. He included both Ernusch and me in his acknowledgements. I quote an excerpt from his statement of recognition.

As a member of the Mennonite family I want to thank you for constantly emphasizing that in the work of MCC, Scripture is our authority. Not expediency. Not government. Not programmes. One of your co-workers in Akron who for many years was close to you summarized your contribution in this way: "Siegfried not only kept the needs of suffering people preeminent, but challenged the staff and Board not to let any cause get in the way of our one purpose—serving in the name, the spirit and style of Christ." You knew so well that one with God is a majority. And that is why you were not afraid to stand alone when your conscience required you to do so. . . .

As a member of the Mennonite constituency I have appreciated your emphasis that MCC is not a para-church organization. MCC is our church at work. And therefore, you urged that the organization remain accountable to the church for all its programmes and activities. . . . I thank you for your careful listening to the heartbeat of our churches.

And this evening I want to recognize that you, Erna, were a vital part of the team. Many of us know the kind of partnership that exists between you and Siegfried. It is said that iron sharpens iron. How often was it that Siegfried was able to clarify a situation or lighten a burden by discussing it with you. You were careful to guard confidences in delicate matters. You were generous with your love and care also in freeing Siegfried to carry the load of leadership.

That meeting marked the end of an era for both Ernusch and me.

VI

Working in the Second Level of MCC

The voices on MCC Canada were not always united. Representatives from the various conferences were not always agreed in their positions on different issues. . . . But the beauty of that board was that conflicting positions on issues did not affect personal relationships. . . .

I was out of province —that means, of course, away from the farm —for approximately 160 days on MCC Canada business.

45. For Whom Do I Speak?

When I became chairperson of MCC British Columbia in November 1971, I automatically became a member of the MCC Canada board (MCCC). I took my position at the board table for the first time at the annual meeting on January 14-15, 1972, in Manitoba.

That board of 33 members consisted of representatives from ten different conferences Canada-wide, five chairpersons of provincial MCCs and several members-at-large. I was board member for as long as I was chairperson of MCC B.C. (1972-1987) and on its executive committee from 1974-1980.

The constitution of MCC Canada stated that "the purpose of MCCC shall be . . . to act as a *united* (italics mine) voice for the Canadian Mennonite and Brethren in Christ churches in matters of national concern, such as peace witness, alternative service, government contracts, immigration and such other matters as may be designated to it by member conferences or organizations." But the voices on MCC Canada were not always united. Representatives from the various conferences were not always agreed in their positions on different issues.

One example was a crucial debate on capital punishment which came early on in my time with MCC Canada. Voting on that issue demonstrated in a dramatic way the dilemma of having one elected member speaking for thousands in the constituency. At the MCC Canada table I represented approximately 15,000 members from Mennonite churches in B.C. (Conference of Mennonites and Mennonite Brethren). Several surveys indicated that the majority of church members in B.C. favoured capital punishment. Yet with my deep conviction on the issue, I clearly and unapologetically took the opposite position

46. The Vote on Capital Punishment

Capital punishment was only one of many issues on MCCC's multi-faceted agenda which took hours of board time and which caused me a lot of agony. Coming to the position where I strongly believed that capital punishment was wrong had been a long process. My convictions on the topic had been shaped partly by a paper written by Frank C. Peters entitled, "Capital Punishment: A Christian Perspective." In it he wrote:

> As Mennonites we believe that life belongs to God and to Him alone. Since we cannot create life we have no right to destroy it. As children of God who condemn the murderer in the name of God for destroying a human life, we cannot turn around and purposely do the same thing ourselves. . . .
>
> As Mennonites we have shown a deep reverence for human life. Such reverence is worth more than a thousand executions in the interest of preventing murder. . . . The law of capital punishment, while pretending to support this reverence, does in fact tend to destroy it. How dare we express our horror and disapproval that a murderer has killed an innocent victim by killing that murderer?
>
> As a Christian I must opt for rehabilitation. This does not mean mandatory parole for those who show no signs of remorse. However, as one who really believes that "where sin abounds, grace does the more abound," I cannot but place myself on the side of mercy and forgiveness.

While I was coming to terms with that issue, I was disturbed by statistics which showed that the attitudes of evangelical Christians were little different than those of Canadians generally: 68 percent called for a return of the death penalty; 20 percent were opposed.

Besides Peters' paper, several factors influenced my position of opposing capital punishment: one was the possibility of a wrong judgement; the other was my own experience.

History has shown that people have been wrongly accused of crimes. One instance involved John Diefenbaker, former Prime Minister of Canada. In his autobiography, *The Crusading Years,* Diefenbaker "recounted how he defended a philandering Russian immigrant accused of murdering another man's wife. The man maintained his innocence throughout the trial, was convicted and hung. Several years later, the real murderer, the woman's husband, confessed on his death bed" (Kevin Jardin, *Accord*, May 1987, 12).

A more recent case in point was Donald Marshall, Jr., the 31-year-old Micmac Indian from Cape Breton, who served 11 years for a murder he did not commit and who was granted $220,000 in compensation from the Government of Nova Scotia. If capital punishment would have been the law in Canada, he would have been executed.

For me the most persuasive argument was based on my experience. Earlier I referred to the "darkest hour of my life," the day when I gave the order to have a young man in Russia executed. It is one thing to have the authority and give the order to execute someone; it is another matter to actually *do* it! If I would have had to pull the trigger, that man would be alive today, perhaps a grandfather like me.

MCCC board members were ready to hear about and try to understand my experiences, but they could not know fully the depth of my struggles. By the time a resolution on capital punishment was presented to the January 1973 MCCC annual meeting, my position was clear. I could agree wholeheartedly with the MCC statement. It considered the question, "Is capital punishment a deterrent?" and came out on the side of saying, "A much greater deterrent, or a responsibility, which all should consider is an entire change in direction in terms of values, ethics, and future outlook."

After considering several biblical passages, the statement said that, rather than punishment, "we should be willing to use our creative means to rehabilitate the offender." It concluded by saying that:

> Mennonites have a history, from our beginning, of objection to capital punishment. As such we have attempted to remain consistent and faithful to the principles we hold as correct. . . . As Christians we want to testify to the sacredness of human life. We confess our acceptance of the Lordship of Jesus Christ, whose will, as we understand it, is not to kill; we can not kill anyone, nor can the state or sub-Christian society, without violating Yahweh's Lordship.

All I could say to that was "Amen!" The motion to request the Canadian Government to abolish the death penalty passed by a 19 to 5 majority vote. The five dissenting votes were from representatives of five different conferences. The beauty of that board was that conflicting positions on issues did not affect personal relationships.

47. Inter-Office Relations

For many years a highly contentious issue had been the working relationship between the MCC Canada (Winnipeg) office and the binational office in Akron. As a member of both executive committees, I found that situation difficult. Frank Epp on the MCC Canada board was promoting a strengthened MCC Canada. For a while, even an independent Canadian MCC was being considered.

The main impetus for that way of thinking was U.S. involvement in the Vietnam War. Antagonism toward the United States of America and the restrictions which were placed on MCC because it was a U.S.-based agency nurtured the position. The majority of executive committee members, representatives from MCC Canada included, pleaded that the overseas work continue to be administered through the binational MCC.

Sometimes Frank Epp criticized Canadians on the MCC executive committee. That extremely gifted man, who had done so much for the Mennonite church worldwide, that apostle of peace on the international scene, was sometimes very forceful in presenting his personal convictions.

I was among those who was deeply convinced that MCC's overseas work should be administered from the Akron office. When a decision had to be made to add buildings at the headquarters in Akron, I made the motion that we proceed with the project. Despite my action, the majority of U.S. staff in Akron did not understand the Canadian position. It was the same there as it is in society at large. Powerful majorities seldom even try to understand minorities, whether that be the attitude of the United States toward Canada, Canada toward Quebec or the aboriginal people, Akron toward Winnipeg, or the General Conference Mennonite Church (Newton) toward the Conference of Mennonites in Canada (Winnipeg).

The deep rift between the two MCCs (Akron and Winnipeg) in regard to the acceptance of government funds for overseas programs was understandable. We Canadians fully accepted the reservations which our U.S. board members and staff had in regard to U.S. government funds. The United States was seen, at least in the third world, as aggressive and dominating. If they contributed to a certain program, there would be strings attached to fall into line with U.S. foreign policy.

We in Canada experienced a completely different approach by our Government. When MCC Canada received large grants from CIDA (Canadian International Development Agency), our international involvements increased. At that time, if the MCC board strongly favoured acceptance of those funds—and senior staff members in Akron were very reluctant to do so—the development of strained staff relationships was inevitable. That somewhat arrogant attitude in Akron was hard to accept by MCC Canada. Other issues also created tensions, but the main areas of disagreement had their roots in that struggle.

Elmer Neufeld, who became chairperson of MCC after the death of Newton Gingrich in 1979, was an exception. He tried hard to understand the Canadian position and contributed significantly to the "Memorandum of Understanding" which was eventually adopted by the two boards.

48. An MCC Presence in Ottawa

A very different issue which occupied our board and executive committee meetings in those years was the question, "Should we as MCC Canada establish an office in Ottawa?" I had never been convinced that the MCC Washington office was clearly an assignment "in the name of Christ." I detected a strong anti-government stand there. At the time I did not realize that Mennonites in the United States had a different relationship with their Government.

Mennonites in Canada had closer ties with their Members of Parliament (as I had experienced in the Doukhobor situation), so I opposed the establishment of an MCCC office in Ottawa. At the annual meeting in January 1974 in Edmonton, Alberta, J.M. Klassen, then Executive Secretary of MCCC, presented a paper in favour of such an office. I delivered the opposite position.

I based my opposition on several arguments. First, I could not see that the usefulness of the Washington office applied in the Canadian situation. Our office in Winnipeg had well established lines of communication both with our Mennonite constituency and with all government departments. I felt that representation from Canadian Mennonites should be made by our "elected" representatives. Also, the argument that an Ottawa office would be an observation and listening post did not seem relevant in our time of modern media.

I felt that the establishment of an Ottawa office with general MCC funds would be poor stewardship. In closing my presentation, I said:

> It is not the intention of this paper to say that we as Mennonites should not speak to political issues. This is the duty and privilege of every responsible citizen, and therefore every church member should be more concerned. If it is necessary that MCC (Canada) should witness in the name of the Mennonites in Canada, as is the mandate for MCC, it is therefore no problem to arrange those meetings from our Winnipeg office. . . .
>
> MCC is one area where most of our Mennonite conferences have found a common denominator. An Ottawa office could well serve

as a wedge in our conferences. The thing that has caused MCC to find such wide acceptance by government and by people of other religions is that we were not politically orientated and involved.

The money and energy that would be spent for such an office should be used more wisely, i.e., MCC relief work. The decision to leave the organizational structure as it is now would help maintain the unity in our brotherhood.

J.M. Klassen then presented forceful arguments *in favour* of an Ottawa office. His rationale was "based on the belief that individual Christians and congregations ought to be aware of what the Government of Canada is doing or planning to do and seek to influence the government to pursue a course of action that most nearly approaches the biblical role of governments (Romans 13).

"The question is not so much whether or not a Christian is or should be involved in politics but how this involvement is best expressed and what direction his influence should take," he said, and then asked, "Who will interpret the Lord's will to the legislators of our land if it is not the Christian church?"

That turned out to be one of the issues on which J.M. Klassen's quiet diplomacy provided significant leadership within MCC. His arguments were convincing and the Ottawa office became a reality. The opposition within our constituency to that step was sometimes painful. A few churches withdrew their support. For them the view that "MCC Canada is too political" seemed verified.

The fact that MCCC found William (Bill) Janzen to be the staff person for the Ottawa office was a special gift of God to MCC and to all Mennonites in Canada. His intelligence, his uncompromising honesty, his deep dedication to Christ and to his church made Bill a highly respected spokesperson for Mennonites in Ottawa.

Even though I had opposed the establishment of this office, when MCC Canada later reviewed its effectiveness, I happily made the motion at the annual meeting to acknowledge Bill Janzen's good work and to continue with that office for the future.

49. Submission to the Deschenes Commission

The only time that I was directly involved in a presentation by MCC Canada to the Canadian Government was the submission to the Deschenes Commission on October 30, 1985. After the Second World War, former citizens of Germany and people of the occupied countries who were involved in war crimes had scattered over the whole world. Britain's Commonwealth Relations Office sent a telegram to Canada and six other Commonwealth governments on July 13, 1948. The British Government decided to suspend further prosecutions of suspected Nazi war criminals in the United Kingdom.

Westminster wanted the Commonwealth allies to adopt the same policy. The punishment of war criminals, the British Telegram noted, "is more a matter of discouraging future generations than of meting out retribution to every guilty individual. . . . So far, the Commission has sifted through allegations that as many as 660 war criminals may be living in Canada." After 1948 the Government of Canada accepted the position of the British Government. However, when Brian Mulroney became Prime Minister of Canada in 1984, that changed and he appointed Justice Deschenes to review those cases.

I was asked by the MCC Canada executive committee to accompany Bill Janzen in our presentation to that Commission. It was suspected that Jacob Luitjens, one of our Vancouver church members, might be on that list. I had special interest in the issue and was familiar with the history of that time. I will let Bill Janzen pick up the story. In his report to the MCCC executive committee on November 6, 1985, he wrote:

> I had sent the background paper to [the Commission], not as a formal submission, but to indicate the kind of concerns we wanted to discuss. . . . The meeting had been scheduled for half an hour but went considerably longer. By way of introduction I referred to MCCC and to the Mennonite people, noting that some have historical roots in Germany and the Soviet Union and therefore have direct experience with war.
>
> Of Siegfried Bartel, I said he had served in the German Army in spite of the historic Mennonite teaching against military service. . . . I then introduced our concern, stating that we wanted primarily to ask that the idea of mercy be considered as having some relevance to the issue. . . .
>
> After this Siegfried Bartel spoke. He said that he had served approximately eight years in the German army, that he had been wounded twice, once in France and once on the Russian front, that he had lost a brother in Russia, and that at the time military service had not bothered him, that he had felt he was doing right, even as a Christian, just like many evangelical Christians today see no problem with military service. Now he was a convinced pacifist, he said.
>
> He restated our view that we were not appealing on behalf of mass murderers like those at concentration camps, that our concern

was with the actions of soldiers and "borderline" cases. He said that in war human life means nothing to either side, that "the more you destroy and kill, the greater a hero you are," and that people coming forty years later in a peaceful situation should be very cautious about judging. . . .

Siegfried then referred to the selectivity issue, noting that major war crimes had also been committed in the Allied bombing of Dresden and the sending back into Russia, after the war, of thousands of Germans from Russia, who had returned to Germany with the retreating German army. . . .

Siegfried then referred to the guilt complex, that is, the inner suffering of people who had served in the German army. He pointed to the way people from the west had condemned them and also to the fact that some had done things about which they could talk to no one and from which they could not be released. (He also knew of people who had served in the Allied forces who suffered such guilt.) . . .

Siegfried concluded his remarks by referring to the message that President Reagan had tried to convey with his Bitburg visit, namely that forty years is enough. He then referred to the phrase in the Lord's prayer: "Forgive us our trespasses as we forgive those that trespass against us." He said that should be our approach.

By way of conclusion, I restated our main concern, namely that the idea of mercy be taken into account in dealing with war criminals even if only in a limited way. Siegfried then told the story of how, when he was seven years old, his mother had been killed in a train accident because the man operating the switches on a railway had been drunk. At the trial his father had pleaded with the judge not to sentence the man. Meighen and Fortier asked, "Did the judge respect that plea?" Siegfried answered yes.

Mr. Fortier then turned to Siegfried and said: "I sense that you have come to terms with your earlier involvement and that you are at peace. You have given us a sense of that peace and we thank you." They said they had found it an "inspiring" meeting.

Unfortunately, the case of Jacob Luitjens was the only one with which the courts proceeded on the recommendation of the Deschenes Commission. After the 1988 court case in Vancouver, it took the Federal judge 29 months to make a decision and recommend to the Federal Cabinet that Luitjens be stripped of his Canadian citizenship.

Surely the way the Canadian courts and the Government of Canada have proceeded has nothing to do with justice. It has to do with politics, and Jacob Luitjens is paying the price. Could Bill Janzen and I, could MCCC have done more to influence the government? All we could say is, "We tried our best!"

50. How Does MCC Share the Gospel?

One very important issue which affects all levels of MCC, in fact, all areas of church work, is the concern about spirituality. John H. Redekop, long-time MCCC board member, focused the concern in April 1988 when he wrote:

> When the Mennonite Central Committee was established after World War I, it undertook several important tasks not then being carried out by evangelism and missions agencies. Christian ministry was thus expanded by all the participating conferences. The evidence indicates that church members and leaders widely supported both evangelism/missions and practical service/peacemaking as expressions of the Great Commission. Since then, particularly in recent years, the situation has deteriorated (*Mennonite Brethren Herald*, April 15, 1988, 12).

John went on to note that some church leaders and members were changing their thinking about MCC and about the Anabaptist peace position because MCC had expanded the peace teaching to include "advocacy in the courts, concern about Native land claims, publicity about ecology, criticism about military bases and militarism, and education concerning exploitation of women." They also objected to the tendency of some ardent MCC defenders to redefine "the practical expression of the gospel" as being "a new whole."

That concern was picked up very forthrightly several months later in a July 29, 1988, MCCC news release with the headlines: "Answer the critics: Does MCC share the gospel?"

> Yes, says MCC. But some members of Mennonite and Brethren in Christ (BIC) churches don't seem so sure. Questions about MCC's commitment to sharing the gospel continually dog the agency. This summer, the subject was raised again at three Mennonite conference conventions. Delegates asked about MCC's interest in evangelism and questioned the faith commitment of volunteers.
>
> MCC Canada Executive Director Daniel Zehr wonders what MCC has to do to convince people that volunteers are committed Christians who share their faith in a variety of ways. "Many people don't know that MCCers work with mission agencies and local churches in evangelism and outreach-related assignments in North America and overseas, as well as working in relief and development," he says.
>
> Why isn't the message getting through? "Maybe we're doing a poor job of telling people about the ways that MCCers share their

faith," he suggests. "As staff we see it happening all the time. Maybe we take it for granted."

But there's another reason, says Zehr. . . . From its beginning in 1920, MCC was mandated to carry out the practical aspects of Christian mission, while the task of church-planting and nurture was left with mission agencies and home mission boards. . . .

"We have a broad constituency," says Reg Toews, [MCC Associate Executive Secretary] "ranging from conservative to liberal and everything in between. There's no one right way to share the gospel. MCCers share it the way they have been taught. The important thing is that we share it."

In regard to the concern about spirituality in MCC board discussions, I often identified more with representatives of the Mennonite Brethren and the more conservative Mennonite groups than I did with my own General Conference people. I found it painful when some of the conservative groups withdrew from MCC because they felt it focused too much of its energy on political issues. On that point I did not agree with them. I had been guilty of not speaking out against injustices in the past and did not want to repeat that mistake.

Does MCC share the gospel? To that question I could wholeheartedly say, "Yes!" As Newton Gingrich stated so well, "MCC does not first stand for bread, but for the Gospel."

51. Responsibility to Canada's Native People

No other area of concern was more important to me during my years on MCC Canada than the fundamental principle that we needed to be a Christian presence to the poor and needy in our own communities. Many in our churches accepted that we should be concerned about poverty in the third world, but they were much more cautious about responding to the needs of the poor in Canada.

I realized that it was easy for us in the white middle or upper class to let our success-oriented philosophy of life overshadow our interpretation of Christ's teaching. But I also felt strongly that without a practical message of love for our neighbours, concerns about bringing the gospel of love to needy people overseas lacked credibility.

In his caring way, Menno Wiebe, Director of Native Concerns for MCCC, kept reminding us of the task of the church of Jesus Christ, of our Christian responsibility to the native people in Canada. That task was not always easy. In fact, the work was often criticized, as happened in an evaluation of the MCCC Native Concerns program as part of a 1980 task force of the Board of Spiritual Concerns of the Canadian MB Conference. The task force report acknowledged "the great, often sacrificial, efforts put forth by Menno Wiebe and his associates working in the area." It also agreed that "a new trust and credibility" had been established between Native people and the church and "we want to give credit where credit is due." The report went on to say:

> But we also feel compelled to emphasize that establishing credibility and good communication, while being praiseworthy in their own right, cannot serve as the ultimate goals of a Christian ministry.
>
> There appears to be some serious questioning in parts of the MCC constituency about MCC's involvement in Indian land claims, northern development, pollution, and related matters. Here, again the situation is complex and priorities can become distorted, but hear the words of Rev. Stan McKay, Jr., a spokesman for the Cree and a former Manitoba moderator of the United Church of Canada. "We face the problem of death because our land is dying. Theologizing about the land is very necessary for my people. Our sense of God is that of a caring, saving, strengthening God; a God who would not have us live without the things we need." . . .
>
> Before we dismiss too quickly the propriety of at least some MCC involvement with native economic and land concerns we do well to ponder McKay's comments as well as the slowly uttered and carefully chosen words of another native spokesman, "If you're hungry, you can't think."

I was never directly involved in MCCC's work with Native Concerns. But I believed strongly that in that area MCC also needed to be "a Christian resource for meeting human need." Our help was to be given "in the name of Christ," not on the basis of some humanistic principle.

52. End of Service

In fall 1987 my involvement with the board of MCC Canada came to an end. At the annual meeting, after 16 years of service, I was among five others who were recognized for "contributions to the ongoing ministry of MCCC." The statement of recognition read:

> They have been an intimate part of our mutual struggles to make wise decisions on the great variety of issues which confront MCCC.

We have prayed together; we have admonished and affirmed one another. In the process we have been drawn closer together as brothers and sisters in Christ. In many cases we have become close friends. In all the give-and-take of serving on the board together, a rapport has developed among us which has lowered the barriers of geography and conference affiliation which sometimes separate us.

In a special card given to me at the 1987 annual sessions of the Conference of Mennonites in Canada in Clearbrook, Larry Kehler, then General Secretary, asked, "Can you count the hours and days, Siegfried, that you have spent reading MCC reports in the last 16 years?"

I calculated that I was out of province—that means, of course, away from the farm—for approximately 160 days on MCC Canada business.

VII

Moving beyond Canadian Boundaries with MCC

My question was: "Could I really contribute anything to this highest level of MCC?" . . . Often on my day-long flights home from executive committee meetings in Akron, Pennsylvania, I asked myself whether the high travel expense and my personal time involvement could be justified. . . . The conviction that I had represented not only myself but many others in the Mennonite constituency made my departure from MCC less painful. . . . They had been good years. Most of the time I felt that the executive members accepted me and took my concerns seriously.

53. Withholding My Vote

My commitment to MCC did not stop with the provincial and Canadian organizations. As chairperson of Mennonite Central Committee B.C., I not only automatically became a member on the MCC Canada board but also on the binational MCC board which had its headquarters in Akron, Pennsylvania. That board had 33 representatives from ten different Mennonite and Brethren in Christ conferences in the United States and Canada.

I attended my first annual meeting in January 1972. My question was, "Could I really contribute anything to this highest level of MCC?" It took a few years for me to learn about and grasp all the issues dealt with in the far-reaching agenda. At the 1975 annual meeting I first experienced a situation in which I did not agree with the majority and decided to abstain from voting on that issue.

In the aftermath of the Vietnam War and Brother Atlee Beechy's visit to North Vietnam, a recommendation was made that MCC send $31,000 to North Vietnam to rebuild a school in one of the villages. I opposed the motion in principle because there was no way to control or supervise the flow of money for that particular purpose.

Funds had been donated by church members in the United States for use in North Vietnam. It seemed to me that, with those donations, our U.S. brothers and sisters were trying to counteract the terrible grief which their country had brought to the people of North Vietnam. I thought the board was naive to believe that a dictator-style government, which had been at war with the country where that money originated, would honestly follow any guidelines for use of funds. I as a Canadian abstained from voting on that motion.

Not all Canadian board members agreed with my position. That was another issue on which MCC Canada Executive Secretary J.M. Klassen and I held opposing views. In response to an article in *Die Mennonitische Rundschau*, a Winnipeg-based, German-language paper, J.M. wrote on April 27, 1977:

> Some people feel that MCC should not help the Vietnamese to reconstruct schools because students will be taught Communism in these schools. It is quite possible that we would have difficulty with

parts of their curriculum or with the biases in their textbooks. But the Vietnamese asked for help to reconstruct schools. Should we withhold our contribution or make it conditional on what they would teach?

A year after the vote on the Vietnam issue, at the 1976 MCC annual meeting, Peter J. Dyck, then MCC director for Europe-North Africa, presented a paper on "Cash and Material Aid without MCC Personnel." He wrote:

> The question arises whether it is possible to disperse funds and distribute material aid without the presence of MCC personnel and still be "an integral part of our mission outreach." The *MCC Handbook* says that MCC's "program is unapologetically a Christian ministry." And again, "it is hoped that both personnel and program can serve as a channel for healing and reconciliation in a broken and divided world."
>   Is there a gap between the ideal and the real, and if so, how big is it? What causes it? Is it reason for alarm? Is it inevitable and perhaps even desirable in certain circumstances?

Dyck then went on to cite examples of MCC doing both: sending aid with and without supervisory personnel. During the 1920s in Russia, distribution of food and clothing was accompanied by MCC persons. After the Second World War, the massive material aid shipments to Germany "were distributed with only very slight American supervision." In Algeria from 1962-1973, the "distribution was closely supervised." Dyck listed six locations where material aid had been distributed in 1975 by "non-MCC channels, mostly without MCC supervision:" $640,000 worth of food and other material aid in Brazil; $70,000 worth of food and clothing through the Coptic Church in Egypt; $28,000 worth of corn in Honduras; $7,000 worth of medical supplies in Lesotho; $34,000 worth of food, clothing and medical supplies in Malawi; and $60,000 worth of milk in Vietnam.
I still was not convinced that was a wise thing to do.

54. MCC and Europe

One result of my intense involvement in the discussion on funds was my election to the MCC executive committee, a position I held for 12 years. That gave me a voice in decision-making at the highest level of MCC.

Until that time Peter J. Dyck was the sole and undisputed authority on Europe. He had come to his assignment during the Second World War under the umbrella of, and in close consultation with, the Allied forces. He had arrived in Germany in 1945. By acknowledging the wonderful work of C.F. Klassen, Peter J. Dyck and many others who worked in Europe in "the name of Christ" and on behalf of all Mennonites in North America, were connected somehow to the victory aspect of the war. We—and I speak as a German—are still thankful for all they did for us, the "condemned" losers of the War.

Hand in hand with the condemnation of a nation was naturally the judgement on Mennonites in Germany who had been fully "Germanized" at that time in history. So it came as no surprise to me that Peter J. Dyck wrote in his report to the MCC executive committee on September 14-15, 1979:

> When there is lack of vision or courage to build the future, a nation, like a person, can always try to resurrect the past and live on that, especially when that past is as strong and colourful as Germany's Prussia once was. For thirty years now Prussia has been a dirty word in Germany, but there are indications that may be changing. Some observers see this as a search for identity, for nationhood. . . .
>
> It will be interesting to observe the Umsiedler's [resettler's] reaction to all this resurrection of the past. With their own roots somewhat in Prussia, though before that they had been in Holland, and more recently in Russia, and especially with their own authoritarian style of family and church life, it could strike in them a welcome and familiar chord.

In using the phrase, "for thirty years now Prussia had been a dirty word in Germany," Peter spoke the language of the victorious nations, in no way the language of the people in Germany. When I joined the MCC executive committee, a different interpretation of the German perspective and of Mennonites in Europe came about.

At that time, it was not clear what MCC's role in Europe should be, as was evident from a document written for a November 1979 consultation at Thomashof by Samuel Gerber, Swiss elder statesman:

> There have been and certainly continue to be all kinds of misunderstandings among the European Mennonites in regard to the role and purpose of MCC. One observes again and again that many European Mennonites believe MCC is the top church organization for all North American Mennonites. And then there are some really comical opinions, as if North American Mennonites represented a

In conversation with Franz Esau of Emmendingen at an MCC consultation on November 19-20, 1979, in Thomashof, West Germany; (in centre background): H.H. Dick, Mennonite Brethren representative. Photo: Lydia Penner

homogenous bloc, which has undertaken a kind of imperialist advance to reform and dominate European Mennonites. . . .

From my personal perspective I can only say that MCC has accomplished an enormous amount in its 30 years of activity in Europe. Certainly mistakes have been made. Many MCC workers have paid dearly for the lessons they learned. But through the channel of MCC the American brotherhood has brought invaluable material aid to Europe. And what is even more important is the personal contact with relief workers and that a number of Europeans were invited to visit American churches. Many North American Mennonites have contributed decisively to the shaping of our faith, through their own examples of faith, their Christian service and through intensive conversations.

The MCC interpretation of the European connection did not come until later when Walter Sawatsky was named as MCC director in Europe. Walter had spent a number of years studying and doing research at Keston College in London, England. He had worked on his PhD thesis, "Soviet Evangelicals since World War II," and had made many trips to Russia.

In evangelical circles, Walter certainly was *the* authority on European and Russian Mennonites. But a gifted researcher with a high intellect is not necessarily the ideal person for administering an MCC program. Nevertheless, Walter did win the full confidence and praise of university-trained Mennonite leaders in Europe. That was not quite the case with lay leaders. It is a rare gift when highly intelligent scholars can relate well to lay people.

In a report to the December 1985 executive committee meeting, Walter presented a very perceptive analysis of why European Mennonites both "seek cooperation with MCC" and resist "cooperation with MCC." He said that Europeans affirmed the partnership aspect of sharing staff and funds. But they remained resistant to the perception that "MCC rules the world. . . . In the end MCC remains the big elephant whose trumpet frightens mice, even if it is playing, 'We are one in the Spirit!'" From my discussion with German Mennonite leaders, I concluded that Walter's observations were correct.

One area where Akron staff and I had some differences in vision in Europe was the combined assignments of MCC with the Eastern Mennonite Board of Missions (Salunga). A joint East-West scholarship program which provided study assistance in Eastern Europe had been in existence for some time. In a June 1981 report, Walter Sawatsky wrote: "We have been assuming a maximum size of a dozen persons. . . . At present MCC personnel are located in Poland, Romania, Hungary with Salunga personnel in West Berlin, Yugoslavia and Bulgaria. Further appointments in Poland, Hungary, and perhaps Romania are anticipated in the near future."

At the time, budget restraints were forcing MCC to cut relief work in the third world, but study assistance in Eastern Europe was to be increased. Eventually, the program was to include 35 persons with a budget of almost $250,000, an increase of $105,000. I expressed my opposition to the excessive increase in that program in a letter to Edgar Stoesz on April 10, 1983:

> I do not question the value of those study programs, and I do not hesitate in believing that some of those brethren [who are receiving funds] may be exceptional gifts from the Lord to our brotherhood. But I cannot accept MCC assistance for all those "exceptions" for potentially future MCC workers without a policy. . . .
> Since the budget cuts were so drastic in other fields, and I had raised the aforementioned question a number of times before, I felt I had to raise it again at the board session.
> Since I found the answers to my questions unsatisfactory, I could not honestly vote in favour of the budget.

Senior staff was concerned about my role as an executive member if I could not vote for the budget at an annual meeting because of lack of a clear policy statement. After the meeting I received a letter of apology from Edgar Stoesz and Reg Toews for not giving better answers to my questions, asking me to clarify my concerns. As a result of that letter exchange, I realized that staff, especially those two, did take the position of executive committee members seriously.

55. Participation in Peace Demonstrations

One very different area of concern regarding MCC work in Europe was the participation in peace demonstrations by MCC staff. The publicity of that action brought strong criticism, mainly from the newly established Umsiedler churches and their leaders and from Mennonites in our North American constituency. Those voices echoed my apprehension.

David E. Redekop, a Mennonite Brethren representative on MCC Canada at the time, expressed his concern in the 1982-83 annual report to his conference in this way: "We support MCC in its stand against all killings, militarism and war. However, we do not support protest marches and also make a distinction between nuclear developments as such and nuclear weapons."

I had raised the issue at the March 1982 executive committee meeting. Consequently, Walter Sawatsky wrote to Edgar Stoesz on April 16, 1982:

> The news service report on the March meeting states that Siegfried Bartel expressed concern about an MCC person in Germany participating in the October 10 peace demonstration in Bonn without the approval of European Mennonite church leaders. Since my article on that demonstration and my involvement in it circulated very widely, informed readers immediately knew who was meant. If there was negative reaction from a specific European Mennonite leader which Siegfried Bartel has information about, I would have expected him to have shared that with me. Perhaps this is only his personal concern and other Executive Committee members feel very differently. Obviously I as staff person need to work in open communication with you and with the committee.

I continued drawing attention to the sensitivities of the Umsiedler Mennonites in Germany on the peace issue. But at the September

1983 executive committee meeting a motion was passed "that Mennonite Central Committee continue to encourage workers in Europe in their peace witness." The motion acknowledged that sensitivity was needed as to which were "appropriate forms of witness" and that "discernment with co-workers" in peace groups was essential.

I was not satisfied. All I could do to indicate my displeasure was state my position again. On October 12, 1983, I wrote to Reg Toews with a copy to Walter Sawatsky:

> I want to clarify one most important point. There is no difference at all in the peace position "in spirit and sharing concern." I become uneasy when so often in discussions the issue of the peace position has been confused with the method of dealing with that position.

Needless to say, sorting through that dialogue was confusing. What hurt me most was that my opposition to demonstrations as a sign of protest was seen as a weakness in my peace position. The

Members of the MCC Executive Committee at the June 1983 meeting in Akron (seated from left): John A. Lapp; Larry Kehler, secretary; Ross Nigh, vice-chairperson; Marie Wiens, Siegfried Bartel; (standing): Lamar Fretz; Joe Neufeld; Florence Driedger; Elmer Neufeld, chairperson; Reg Toews, executive secretary; Bruce Harder, Paul Landis; Norman G. Shank. Photo: Mark Beach.

reader will know by now that that interpretation was absolutely wrong. I had one deep concern in my many discussions on peace issues: that the true peace position was measured not on one's willingness to join demonstrations but on whether one's position was biblically based.

56. Assistance to Bruno Schottstädt

I disagreed strongly with MCC's Europe desk on the relationship and financial travel assistance to Bruno Schottstädt, a pastor in East Berlin. That assistance continued over an extended period of time. He had a long list of travel experiences from East Germany to the West at a time when only STASI (an intelligence agency) could recommend the possibility of travel to the West.

Schottstädt's 1981 trip to North America to visit Mennonite schools and conferences was very controversial. Dr. George K. Epp, then president of Canadian Mennonite Bible College in Winnipeg, reported Schottstädt's visit there in a May 8, 1981 letter to MCC Canada's overseas office. He indicated that Schottstädt was "not interested in dialogue" and that he was biassed in his evaluation of the situation in Germany.

After a trip to Germany on May 18, 1990, I once more raised my voice in a letter to John Lapp, Executive Secretary of MCC:

> I learned in Berlin that Bruno Schottstädt is invited to Winnipeg to the MWC [Mennonite World Conference] by invitation of MCC, and that they are financially responsible for the trip. It has been my understanding that his role has been questionable at best, and I think it is irresponsible to finance anything for him.

Schottstädt's relationship to MCC continued during the tenure of four different European MCC directors—and that, in spite of strong criticism and opposition of a large part of the Canadian and German constituencies. Despite my concerns about and opposition to the Schottstädt "love affair," the relationship between him and MCC did not change until East Germany disappeared.

The Schottstädt incident with MCC showed me that I did not have a lot of influence with the organization. That experience taught me one thing—and I am sad that it is so: whatever concerns board or executive committee members might have, if they were critical of plans or budgets presented by senior staff, very few changes would result.

Often, on my day-long flights home from executive committee meetings in Akron, I asked myself whether the high travel expense and my personal time involvement could be justified.

57. Work with Umsiedler

Another area where I did not fully agree with activities in the European MCC program was the withdrawal in 1983 from the *Gemeinsames Gremium*. That organization had been formed by European Mennonites and MCC to assist the Umsiedler who were coming out of the U.S.S.R. Walter Sawatsky took that action because he and Hans von Niessen, staff person for the Umsiedler, had different approaches in dealing with *Umsiedlerbetreuung* (resettler assistance). The move was accepted by the MCC executive committee at the December 16-17, 1983, meeting and was irreversible.

Mennonites from Holland strongly opposed the action. After a stop-over in Europe from February 20 to 23, 1984 (at the end of a trip to South-East Asia), it was clear to me that the flow of immigrants from the Soviet Union—12,000 till then—would increase. Yet I, as the executive committee member who had been involved with John Wieler in establishing the *Umsiedlerbetreuung* organization, had not even been consulted about MCC's withdrawal from the *Gemeinsames Gremium*.

Walter Sawatsky and I visited with various people in Germany and the Netherlands. Walter took notes of a conversation we had with representatives of Dutch Bijzondere Noden (Dutch Special Needs):

> The two Dutch brethren wished to review the decision of MCC to withdraw one step from full membership on the Gemeinsames Gremium. We listened to them and tried to understand their concern. . . . The major point Siegfried made was that MCC continues to support Umsiedler work and will definitely anticipate making a financial contribution beyond 1984 with the amount depending on the need but likely divided 50-50 with IMO [International Mennonite Organization] as earlier. But we do not expect to roll back the decision. If the new smaller Executive involving Umsiedler representatives fails to work, or if many more Umsiedler suddenly come, the MCC will certainly be ready to review the structural arrangements and the level of its assistance.

That unilateral action by MCC characterized the earlier relationship with Mennonites in Europe. I remember French and Swiss Mennonites speaking with some sadness about MCC's diminished participation at the time when IMO was formed in Europe. According to their interpretation they did not join IMO because MCC was not part of it.

Again I was in the minority. I believed that MCC lost a golden opportunity to contribute to the unification of relief work of Mennonites in Europe in three different actions: at the time of establishing IMO; by the unilateral withdrawal from the Gemeinsames Gremium; and by a later decision to relocate the MCC Europe office from Neuwied (Germany) to Switzerland.

58. Back to My Roots

Perhaps this is a good place to add a short aside about another involvement I had in Europe. During six years of my time on the executive committee of MCC, I was also a member on the European Ministries Committee of the Conference of Mennonites in Canada. That committee represented the link between the Canadian Conference to the Mennonite churches in Germany which had a high percentage of Umsiedler from the Soviet Union.

Because of participation on the Conference committee, my trips to Europe on behalf of MCC often included some work for the Canadian Conference. In that joint assignment I visited Germany seven times from 1975 to 1987. Those trips also gave me a chance to get back to my roots and to connect with people in my former homeland.

The main issue for both MCC and the Mennonite conferences in Germany after 1976 was building bridges to the Umsiedler who had emigrated from the Soviet Union to West Germany in the 1970s and 1980s. Whereas MCC's main assignment was to assist German Mennonites in caring for Umsiedler through the *Umsiedlerbetreuung*, the agenda of the Conference of Mennonites in Canada was to work in partnership with Umsiedler congregations through AGUM, the *Arbeitsgemeinschaft zur geistlichen Unterstützung in Mennonitengemeinden* (Working Group for Spiritual Support in Mennonite Congregations). Congregations which joined AGUM had anywhere from 10 to 100 percent of their membership coming from among the Umsiedler. Some of those congregations had long histories; others, such as the churches at Bielefeld, Wolfsburg and the new congregations in Neuwied, had their beginnings after the Umsiedler flow started.

It soon became apparent that the long-standing Mennonite churches in Germany had very little in common with the new arrivals. That's where the Canadian connection came into play. Many Umsiedler families had ties to emigrants who had come to Canada in the 1920s and 1940s. For a number of years, the Canadian Conference, through its European Ministries program, provided pastoral leadership for the Wolfsburg congregation and sent short-term church workers to help with pastoral and teaching work in other congregations. During the time I was involved with the committee, requests by AGUM for help from the Canadian Conference gradually declined.

My seven trips to Germany gave me the opportunity to be a messenger between the Umsiedler and the Canadian Mennonite people and churches. In both the MCC and Canadian Conference assignments, I came into contact with many exceptional people, among them Hans von Niessen. His assignment to work with Umsiedler (*Umsiedlerbetreuung*) was to include *all* Mennonites coming out of the Soviet Union, and he did that faithfully.

In 1990 with Gladys Stoesz, Hans von Niessen and Edgar Stoesz in Neuwied, West Germany.

Nevertheless, they did split up into three different groups. One group joined existing Mennonite churches or formed new ones with the same main principles. Those of Mennonite Brethren background became part of Mennonite Brethren churches in Germany or formed new ones. A third group, people of Mennonite background who had joined Baptist churches in Russia and did not want to be identified as Mennonites, chose not to relate to the Baptists but formed the *Bund Taufgesinnter Gemeinden* (Union of Anabaptist Congregations). This was the largest group of the three groups. Hans von Niessen was perhaps the only church leader who was welcomed by all three (although probably not in participation in the Lord's Supper).

He was very diplomatic in many aspects of his work with and for the Umsiedler, whether it was with all levels of government or with church organizations. He was seen as too evangelical for the majority of Mennonite university-trained theologians, too "modern" for a large number of Mennonite leaders coming out of Russia, too independent in thinking and action for some Umsiedler organizations and some leaders in MCC but, in my appraisal, an exceptional servant of the Lord.

59. Policy on Relief

One continuing area of concern in MCC's overall policy regarding the third world was the evaluation of relief work. Relief—development—justice: "How are these related?" was the big question. In his book, *Bread for the World*, Arthur Simon begins with the words: "Hunger is a child with shrivelled limbs and a swollen belly. It is the grief of parents, or a person gone blind for lack of Vitamin A. A single example of hunger is one too many" (3). In 1974 the United Nations reported that, by most conservative estimates, more than 460 million people were permanently hungry.

How much could one small agency such as MCC do to relieve some of the suffering? A related question, "What can be done so that people are encouraged to help themselves?" concerned the issue of development. And then there was the obvious helplessness about finding the right approach to deal with those questions. Western agencies and governments often used Western-style approaches to third world problems. Some have done more damage than good.

Relief—development—justice. Many books have been written about those three areas of involvement. Genuine searches for answers were pursued, especially in regard to MCC's limited finances and personnel. The "Resolution on World Food Crisis" passed at the 1974 MCC annual meeting in Hillsboro, Kansas, emphasized assistance to the hungry world with food shipments. Some voices within MCC, through the influence of secular organizations, were worried about the heavy increase in food shipments and were afraid that the personal initiative of the receiving people might diminish. I was able to minimize that concern, based on my own experience in Germany after the Second World War. The food that we received when hunger was apparent in many parts of Europe certainly did not hinder our initiative in helping ourselves.

Two slogans which MCC promotes have not always been as clearly visible in some areas of overseas work as we think: "A Christian resource for meeting human need" and "In the name of Christ." When Christians fighting Muslims in Beirut had "In Christ's name" engraved on their weapons, it was questionable whether it would be wise to have "In the name of Christ" stamped on our shipment of beef to Arab refugee camps. That was the only situation where I, as a board member, agreed that the label, "In the name of Christ," should be deleted. That uncompromising position finally did lead to our workers having to leave the state of Israel. In no other circumstances was an action like that discussed during my years with MCC.

60. Learning about MCC in South America

For some time MCC (binational) had the policy of asking executive committee members to accompany country secretaries on their administrative trips. The purpose was to observe overseas activities, to dialogue and strengthen relationships with our workers in the field and to do some pastoral functions. During my 16 years with MCC, I was able to go on two major trips. These trips abroad convinced me that MCC executive committee members should do more travelling to the field. They helped me to understand and make policy decisions based much more on my own views, to relate better to our field staff (North Americans and nationals) and to appreciate the valuable work of our staff.

In 1982 I was invited to accompany Herman Bontrager, Secretary for Latin America, and Edgar Stoesz, Associate Executive Secretary for Overseas Services. The trip began on February 6, 1982, when I travelled to Paraguay with Herman, and ended on February 28 when I returned from Brazil with Edgar.

The purpose of the visit was to become familiar with MCC programs in South America. When it was all over, I understood problems related to programs and could make decisions more wisely.

Paraguay. I was thankful to be able to accompany Herman Bontrager on his administrative visit to Paraguay. His sensitivity to others, his capable and conscientious way of dialoguing, his firm position when he had made up his mind—in all those ways he showed himself to be a humble but highly respected administrator. The Paraguayan schedule was packed. First there was the long drive to the Chaco with all the accompanying adventures on the unpaved part of the Chaco Highway. We found out how heavy the front of the VW Rabbit was—and how muddy the water in the puddles could be.

We visited a health clinic in East Paraguay and the Kilometer 81 Leprosy Hospital in Asuncion. The latter had been established by Paraguayan Mennonites. My second cousin Clara and her husband Dr. John Schmidt had headed up that work for many years. It was good to see them again. We met with many church leaders and *Oberschulzen* (mayors) and with all MCC personnel. I observed the dedication of our workers and experienced their deep commitment to our Lord and to their work. We spent time at the Indian settlement projects and heard, from both Mennonites and some Indian leaders, the call for more organized and stronger leadership. We participated in a peace conference in Loma Plata and the annual meeting of the church board. The peace conference was well attended with wide participation of all church leaders, church workers and missionaries. Peace was a church issue and not an issue discussed by a select group as it probably was in North American Mennonite churches.

In my report on that trip I noted that technical development in the colonies was advancing very fast and that, in general, the outlook for the colonies appeared good. It seemed to me that financial assistance from MCC was necessary only for further Indian settlement activities and perhaps for some mission-related projects.

Uruguay. From Paraguay, I went to Uruguay on my own. Several men were interested in developing a plan to provide more service to the poor in their country. I noted that the future outlook for the Mennonite colonies in Uruguay had improved. But I wondered whether the colonies would be able to keep their identity for more than one more generation.

Brazil. The time in north-eastern Brazil was the most dramatic experience for me. I met Edgar Stoesz in Recife. After a three-hour bus trip to Bonito with Martin and Marian Penner, we drove by motorbike for 20 minutes to the family residence. I was dismayed to see that our MCC workers lived in the same conditions as local farmers or workers. It was sobering to see how happy the family was—even little Timmy who had only one truck to play with. I found it hard to believe that a family of five could live with so little water, yet keep everything so clean and neat. That family's dedication to the work and love for the people was an example to us.

I was at the discussions that Edgar Stoesz had with unit leaders and with leaders of Christian relief agencies in Recife, and met several of the workers. They told of the development of Bible study groups within the Catholic Church. That movement had some parallels with the beginning of the Anabaptist movement of our forefathers.

I met one old brother (approximately 75) who could not read or write, but was able to quote many Bible passages and was actively evangelizing. He sometimes walked two to three hours (one way) over the mountains to lead Bible study groups in other villages. The same movement was active in the *favillas* (shantytowns in the slums). Many workers in north-eastern Brazil were taking part in that "mission project." And people in North America were wondering how MCC was sharing the gospel?

During our visit to Brazil I enjoyed Edgar Stoesz's global approach to issues. I admired his ability in leading discussions even when critical questions were raised, his relaxed way of dealing with leaders of related organizations, and his personal and firm way of giving leadership to our workers. I came away from that trip thinking, "MCC can be thankful to God for our responsible administrators and for our dedicated workers in the field."

The South America visit was a tremendous learning experience for me. After we got home, Herman Bontrager and Edgar Stoesz wrote:

> Just a note to say that we enjoyed having you with us on our recent travels in Latin America. When wisdom based in experience was needed, you rose to the occasion. When comments at the peace conference needed to be challenged, you spoke. When our German was inadequate, you graciously helped. When given a shower of Chaco mud, you were a good sport. When confronted by some new and strange ideas, you exhibited an open mind. In short, your insights were useful, your company enjoyable, and now your more informed support will help to further the work.

61. Seeing MCC at Work in Asia

A second invitation to travel overseas came in an April 8, 1983, letter from Reg Toews. The trip became a reality in winter 1984. On January 29, after two annual meetings—MCC Canada and MCC binational—and a long flight—Vancouver, New York, Zurich, Calcutta, Dhaka—what an adjustment to be in Bangladesh—or anywhere in Asia, for that matter—for the first time. My MCC companion on that trip was Paul Myers, Secretary for Asia.

I had done a lot of reading and had been part of long and intense discussions about Bangladesh and India before we left. One question was on my mind, "Can development be a workable and an effective tool in the ministry of MCC?" I came home with the answer, "Yes, it can!"

Bangladesh. MCC's involvement in Bangladesh was multi-faceted. Our MCC agriculture workers had introduced crops that could be grown outside the normal rice season; for example, soybeans, sweet potatoes, wheat and mustard. That method not only helped the active farmer to produce more food, but also assisted the marginal farmer who was not able to feed his family sufficiently to make a living from his small acreage.

Together with other agencies, MCC had established three villages for landless families on a new formation of land in a river area. Each family received some land for farming. Several female workers had started a gardening program with the women in small villages so that landless people could add some vegetables to their meagre rice diets. Approximately 250 women and 18 supporting staff had been hired to run the Action Bag Handicraft Project. Women, who had been selected on the basis of need, received cash for making jute bags; the balance was banked for them to establish some base for income. Another program for women was quilt-making. MCC bought the material (men's pants) which the women cut up and sewed into quilts in their homes. MCC then purchased the quilts and distributed them to hospitals and orphanages throughout Bangladesh.

Those development projects certainly were providing a ministry. But there was deep concern among some MCC workers that our spiritual nurturing of people with whom we worked was insufficient. One put it this way, "I guess I am not really convinced of the benefit/value of purely development work ... when I think of things on a spiritual, not just on a material level."

Another said, "I still think Christian social action is something all disciples of Christ are called to. But it needs to be part of a holistic program that recognizes multiple aspects of the human condition."

Several other issues came to the fore: Do people become too dependent on MCC through its relief and development work? How can non-Christian national staff in the MCC program best be accommodated?

To the first question, James Pankratz, MCC worker stationed in Dhaka, said, "I think we can help people be more independent than they were before we began to work with them---much of the time." To the second he said, "I think we must work harder at finding settings and methods to at least help staff understand our vision of a reconciled world under the lordship of Christ."

In Bangladesh I also became aware how difficult it was for our female MCC personnel within the Muslim setting. Rosella Toews was one woman who had gone to Bangladesh under the Mennonite Brethren Board of Missions in the early '70s "for one year *only*"---and she was still there!

In reflecting on "Why I stayed in Bangladesh for ten years," Rosella wrote, "It takes time to develop relationships. Through the years some relationships have developed into friendships. I feel like the people accept me now as 'one who belongs'."

I believe everyone should adopt that position in relating to women in the national churches. It would be helpful if female workers in a given setting would accept the culture of the area without trying to impose their North American agendas.

After the Bangladesh trip I felt that MCC should review its commitment to proclaiming the gospel along with a strong emphasis on relief and development work.

India. The program in India differed drastically from that in Bangladesh. For one thing, there was a Mennonite church in India. Although they were having internal difficulties, more Christians were available as national staff. The MCC program was characterized by a strong relief effort, which was visible also through the large Food for Work and the Food for Community Development programs. Excellent work was being done by both groups. I agreed that relief was definitely the number one need in India. As long as children and helpless old people were dying of malnutrition at such magnitude, then there was a mandate for relief efforts.

It would be presumptuous of me to make remarks about India after such a short visit. The words of Marie K. Wiens, an executive committee member who visited India in November 1984, sum up my response:

> India is too much to absorb in so short a time. . . . It could take a lifetime to comprehend what India has been, is and where it is going. The era of the Nizam and the Maharajahs, the caste system, the dowry system, the peace movement which brought about independence and its own brand of violence, the deep hatreds and cruelties of Sikhs and Hindus, but also the goodness and generosity of the Indians—yes, it would take a lifetime.

Pakistan. The visit to Pakistan was different than the other two in that it was informative rather than program-oriented. The huge refugee camps on the border of Afghanistan (and more inside Pakistan) were witness to the war situation. Apparently, the physical need of the refugees was being met. We also saw that the needlework program there was very successful and appreciated.

We left Asia on February 19. It was a joy to see our MCC family——field staff, national staff and country directors——working in those countries "in the name of Christ."

62. Personnel in Contested Areas

Back at the board table, a disturbing question arose at the MCC annual meeting on January 24, 1985: "Should the MCC board endorse the placement of personnel in contested areas?" A three-fold recommendation was presented to delegates for affirmation:

> 1. that we seek new ways to bring the plight of the Salvadoran people and their desire for peace and justice before our constituency, asking them to intercede with our governments on the Salvadorans' behalf. More specifically we want to stand in opposition to policies which deny basic human rights to part of the Salvadoran people because of their desire for changes in the structure of Salvadoran society;
> 2. that we affirm and support two MCC nurses in their call to live and work in two transitional towns in the Morazan and Chalatenango departments. These towns are not controlled by either side in the conflict and, as a result, all people have access to services provided there;

3. that we provide emergency aid on a project basis and through churches and church leaders (food, clothing, health services and agricultural supplies) to people living in contested zones.

That recommendation on El Salvador was accepted. I was the only board member who voted against the motion. Because of my experience in war situations, I could not vote for it. The Central American director's statement which formed the basis for the discussion, warned: "This is a dangerous initiative. Our workers will be perceived as civilians in those areas."

In the discussion on the issue, several situations were given where MCC had sent workers into settings from which they did not return; for example, Clayton Kratz's disappearance in Ukraine in 1920. My point was that critical situations developed *during* the time of service, even though they may not have been considered dangerous when workers were sent out.

A set of guidelines was proposed. In the introduction, it was acknowledged that "behind the analysis, the learnings and the guidelines lies the most important factor—a clear recognition of our dependency on God's Spirit for our security and leading. This sug-

Making a point at the microphone during the January 30-31, 1987, annual MCC meeting in Saskatoon, Saskatchewan. Photo: Bruce Hildebrand

gests that in all of our planning we wait, listen, share and earnestly seek God's direction."

After the January 1985 meeting I seriously considered resigning from MCC. Only because my resignation and the subsequent publicity about my reason for doing so would have done tremendous damage to the MCC program within the constituency, prevented me from going through with it. Marie Wiens who represented the MB Conference, wrote me a letter dated January 31, 1985.

> We just got back yesterday afternoon . . . I felt that you were very quiet during these board meetings. I know it is hard to take a position other than what the rank and file board member does. I have discovered that too, and I don't find it any easier today than when I started.
>
> The purpose of this letter is just to encourage you as a board member. Your kind of voice is needed on that board. Not everyone has the courage to voice his/her convictions. It is always easier to "go along." I wonder what the board will be like when you have served out your term. Hopefully, and it usually happens, others will rise to the occasion, and be a cautioning voice.

Praise the Lord, we did not lose any of our workers and nobody was taken hostage. But the precedent had been set and in 1987 MCC went even further. Delton Franz from the Washington office reported on May 22, 1987:

> The Department of State has determined that the situation in Lebanon has become so dangerous that no U.S. citizen can be considered safe from terrorist acts. In light of this determination the Secretary of State has exercised his authority to invalidate U.S. passports for travel to, in or through Lebanon.

Yet, the following recommendation was accepted by the MCC executive committee: "That we respond positively to the Middle East Council of Churches (MECC) invitation for Carol McLean to serve as a nurse in their community health clinic in Sidon, South Lebanon. Carol supports this response."

Liberation theology was sometimes influential in convincing mainly younger staff members that MCC was called also to "contested areas." But my position remained the same as it was in 1985: it was irresponsible to send people into places which we know to be "contested areas." After all, there were millions of other needy areas where the personal risk to individuals was not the main issue.

I remain convinced that I represented not only my personal position but also that of the largest segment, if not the whole, of the North American Mennonite church community. I am thankful to God that my fear for the workers and their well-being was unfounded. What would have happened if they had been tortured and killed?

63. Policy on Abstinence

Another area where I did not agree with the majority of the executive committee was on the principle of abstinence from the use of alcoholic beverages. A letter to the MCC executive committee from MCCers Justine and David Foxall in Chad on April 25, 1983, brought that question to the agenda.

They indicated, "We are deeply offended by the imposition of a social ethic we do not agree with, that is the statement of clarification in the 1982 Statement of Policy for Overseas Personnel prohibiting the consumption of alcoholic beverages." They continued:

We are offended for the following reasons:
1. We perceive an apparent inconsistency between the policy statement and the clarification which follows. The policy statement, which appears to treat MCC workers as adults, trusts us to be guided by our personal consciences in a way that is pleasing to God, to our local communities and to MCC. The statement of clarification, which appears to treat MCC workers as children, does not show trust in our personal consciences by prohibiting a specific area of behaviour. We think that this is inconsistent with the general tone of MCC's confidence in its workers and its policies regarding worker conduct.
2. We perceive that the rationale for this statement of clarification has been largely developed for the benefit of a certain sector of the MCC constituency. This is not a statement of Christian belief, which would seem to be more important, but it is a statement legislating social behaviour. We feel exploited by the policy makers of MCC who seem to be manipulating our behaviour/consciences in order to please a sector of the MCC constituency.
3. We observe from personal experience within MCC that this statement of prohibition in the policy handbook breeds hypocrisy and resentment which can lead to an undermining of faith in MCC philosophy and policy in general.

My experience regarding alcohol was different than that of most North American Mennonites. I identified with the Foxalls and pleaded for a change. To sign something which the signer knows he or she will not obey is making a mockery of a declaration.

Akron staff had prepared a statement: ". . . it is expected that MCC workers will not purchase or serve an alcoholic beverage or drink one when an alternative is available. MCC workers may participate at work-related socials or ceremonial occasions when an alternative is not available." The majority of executive members favoured deleting the last sentence.

64. Farewell to MCC

In this section I have focused on issues where I had difficulty with "majority decisions"1 where I personally took another stand. There were hundreds of situations where I wholeheartedly endorsed the work of MCC.

The conviction that I had represented not only myself but many others in the Mennonite constituency made my departure from MCC in 1987 less painful. By that time I was by far the oldest executive committee member. We loved each other and enjoyed each other as brothers and sisters in the Lord, but my position was sometimes like "a voice from the past century."

In my 12 years with MCC I attended 48 executive committee meetings and 16 annual meetings. That meant I was out of the province on MCC business (including overseas travel but *not* involvement with MCC Canada) for 280 days.

At the annual meeting in Souderton, Pennsylvania, on January 28-29, 1988, I bade farewell. I was given opportunity to respond to my time of service. The minutes summarize my comments:

> Siegfried told of his earliest memories of MCC, of C. F. Klassen's instructions to not lose a sense of family and to wait and listen for five years before speaking out about life in Canada. (After six years Siegfried became chairman of his congregation.) Siegfried remembered board discussions about relief and development and about involvement in Vietnam. He cautioned MCC to not merely listen to secular thought about development but to always help the poor wherever they are. He also reminded us that MCC's first involvement was to help Mennonite people under a Marxist government. He suggested that MCC is involved in too many countries and he asked MCC to be sure to maintain contact with the smaller Mennonite groups. He concluded with thanks for the quality of relationships he experienced with board members and staff.

Those had been good years. Most of the time I felt that the executive members accepted me and took my concerns seriously. But, as so often happens when a person leaves, it was only after my last meeting that I was sure. A formal resolution indicated:

> We will miss Siegfried's passionate concern, profound faith and clear presentation of a vision. We are grateful for the time and energy Siegfried has devoted to the work of God. We thank Erna Bartel for her willingness to live with many absences, some for an extended period of time.

Executive Secretary John Lapp's follow-up letter stated:

> I have told several people you were the hardest working and most conscientious board member. While I didn't always agree with your point of view, I had to respect your rationale and the way you lived your convictions. We will miss your faithful and selfless service.

A more personal expression came from a brother who had experienced the terrors of war more recently than I. Earl Martin, who was MCC Co-secretary for East Asia, had been in Vietnam for many years. He wrote:

> You know, we're going to miss you, brother. Somehow, I am sad to see you leave the executive committee.
> It's strange. I had heard about you long before we met. As a field worker in Vietnam, we had heard of some of the concerns you raised during some of the decisions about MCC work in North Vietnam. I supposed at that time that I would find myself often not in agreement with many of your views.
> It's strange. Even though we've spent only limited time together over the years, in some ways you have felt a bit like a father to me. One who was strong. One who was courageous enough to express the depth of his convictions. How I have admired that. And yet one who would not stand in the way when the apparent discernment of the body was different from his own. How I would want to emulate that.
> I have often felt that your voice in MCC board and executive committee meetings was the voice of a far larger part of our Mennonite family than the particular conference you represented in Canada. As I got to know you over the years a bit better, I came to understand that, while I did not always agree with Siegfried, no one loved MCC more than Siegfried. No one's service in the name of

Christ anywhere in the world was more complete and committed than Siegfried's.

Another deep spiritual bond I felt with you, Siegfried, was your first-hand experience with the horrors of war. Even though our war experiences were each unique, yet I always felt you understood some things in your bones, in your very soul, that are known only by people who lived many nights uncertain whether they would see the morning, people who have carried a fallen friend in their arms.

And so when you shared your story from the front lines hearing the Christmas carols of Russian soldiers, I was deeply moved. . . .

Brother, your leaving gives us sadness. Surely the stream of God's work through MCC will flow on, but we will miss you. The knowledge that your prayers and the presence of your spirit will continue to uphold us is comforting.

Joy to you, friend, and the peace of God's Spirit as you write your reflections . . .

The time for writing did not come until later, but the encouragement of Earl Martin and others on the MCC executive committee and staff certainly helped keep me going when I actually did sit down to start writing my story.

VIII

Sharing My Story

I've written about what happened to me when I was growing up and while I was at war; about my wonderful family and my experiences in farming; about my struggles with the organized church and my opportunities for service in the wider church setting; about how other people enriched my life during my travels in North America and beyond. . . . But the story yet to be told is how God led me on the path to freedom.

65. The End of Farming

My years with MCC were unforgettable times of interaction and decision-making at the board table, of learning during trips abroad and of fellowship with many people who became my friends. But, meanwhile, back at the farm . . .

When Erna and I moved off the farm at Easter 1979, Martin and Wanda were ready to take over its operation. When we discussed the financial future of Birchlane Farms with our accountant, Barry McKnight, I asked him, "If Martin takes over the farm operation, can he later pay off the share value to his brothers?" Barry stated clearly that he would never be able to do that. When we evaluated Barry's reply, it became clear to both us and Martin that we would be better off selling Birchlane Farms. I found it unacceptable that, all his life, Martin would have to deal with the participation of his brothers as shareholders in the farm.

We decided to put Birchlane Farms on the market and buy a different farm for Martin and Wanda. By that time the value of dairy farms and of milk quotas had risen exorbitantly. All of us—including Martin and Wanda—agreed that selling the family farm would be the best option. In autumn 1980 we put up the "For Sale" sign.

The decision to sell Birchlane Farms sent shock waves through the circles of our relatives and friends. Their feelings were based mainly on pity for Martin and Wanda. Some of them thought the action was unfair for them and told me so. It certainly was not easy for Martin to accept the changed situation, so that reaction of others was not very helpful for him. It was clear from the beginning of our new plan that Martin would buy another smaller farm to operate completely on his own.

Cornelius Klopp saw the "For Sale" sign and came to inquire about the property. He farmed the neighbouring land where he had put up all new buildings and turned his place into a completely modern operation. In the late 1970s he bought the old Tuyttens farm as his second property. Now he wanted to sell both of his farms to buy ours.

For a number of years farms had been selling very well, but during the time of our dealing a different business climate had developed. It

A studio photo shortly before we moved off Birchlane Farms in 1979.

was the beginning of the 1980 recession when interest rates had shot up into the high teens. Cornelius was not able to sell either of his farms. I suggested that we would take the farm in town as trade-in for $400,000.

In the meantime we were looking for a suitable farm for Martin and Wanda. One option would have been for them to take the trade-in farm, but a number of factors discouraged such a move. Rather, we bought the former Wynia farm on Tramner Road.

After it became clear that C. Klopp would not be able to sell his main farm, I made additional concessions. I suggested that for the first five years he could pay us only half the interest; the other half would be added to the principal which he owed as in the agreement for sale. On June 3, 1981, the farm was sold for $1,375,773 with one-third of the milk quota and all unregistered livestock.

Martin took all the purebred cattle, two-thirds of the milk quota and all the machinery. On July 1 he started to operate his own farm on Tramner Road as MarWaBar Holsteins (Martin, Wanda Bartel). With the excellent help of Barry McKnight, our accountant, Martin's one-third share of Birchlane Farms was transferred to MarWaBar. That transaction was to the full satisfaction of everyone involved.

On July 1, 1981, my responsibility as a dairy farmer came to an end: 30 years from the beginning of farming on Dixon Road to the sale of the Birchlane Farms operation. The company, Birchlane Farms Limited, continued to operate the assets belonging to it. For a few years, until I rented it out, I farmed the old Tuyttens farm by growing corn. Later we sold most of the ploughable land.

During the time that Martin and Wanda farmed I offered my assistance to them as I was able and willing. I did the milking chores only in exceptional cases, but I did a lot of tractor driving, mainly during the time of haying and making silage.

Even while he operated his own farm, Martin had always shown strong interest in working with juveniles who needed help. His and Wanda's search for God's will for the future in their lives led them to new decisions. Various circumstances, one being the high interest rates, made farming more and more difficult. So they decided to put up their own "For Sale" sign. When they received no serious inquiries in the first month, Martin and Wanda thought the Lord wanted them to continue farming and did not renew the listing to keep the farm on the market.

One day a friend from church told Martin about an ad in the Chilliwack paper. Someone wanted to buy a dairy farm which would not be listed with a real estate agent. Within a day after Martin contacted the interested people, they showed up at the farm, accompanied by an interpreter. They were of Swiss origin and could speak only French and German. How happy they were when they found out that Martin spoke German. After seeking advice from our accountant and having additional discussions with the bank manager, the farm was sold.

Things moved quickly. Martin and Wanda and their sons moved into the house in town owned by Birchlane Farms. The house on the old Tuyttens farm was renovated and, on April 1, 1989, management of the farm went to the new owner. Martin helped them get acquainted in Agassiz and, on occasion, even acted as interpreter for them.

With the sale of Martin and Wanda's farm our whole family's involvement in farming came to an end. We had no regrets, only joyous memories of hard work, family cooperation and happy, meaningful relationships with very different people over those 30 years.

66. Diary of Preaching-Teaching Assignments

Throughout the years my farming obligations had diminished. The end of our whole family's involvement in farming and my departure from the MCC Canada and MCC binational boards came only a year apart. Surely now I should have time to sit down and write my reflections. But it was not to be.

On January 19, 1988, I received a copy of a letter from Dan Zehr to all the provincial MCC directors. He was asking for their response to the idea that Erna and I visit churches and schools to tell our story. He wrote:

> I have explored with Siegfried and Erna their availability to do some constituency itineration for MCC. They are open to this; but we agreed that I would make their availability known to the provincial MCC organizations before proceeding with definite plans. I think they are quite flexible in terms of when such itineration would take place, but details would obviously need to be checked with them. . . . What they might share:
>
> 1. Siegfried and Erna should be invited to share their story. Theirs is a moving pilgrimage that illustrates from personal experience the call to peacemaking, relief, service, stewardship and God's faithfulness. They have provided Christian parenting to six sons, much of the burden having fallen on Erna, with the strong support and leadership of Siegfried.
>
> 2. With Siegfried's extensive involvements in MCC policy making, he is an able interpreter of what MCC does. He does his homework well, and would utilize effectively documents like reports, minutes, etc. in preparation for public sharing.

After discussing the assignment with Dan, we agreed that Erna would not necessarily always accompany me. She simply did not feel comfortable speaking in public.

The preaching-teaching assignment began on November 11, 1988, with participation at the MCC Saskatchewan annual meeting in Rosthern, Sask. Beginning that assignment on Remembrance Day with a personal testimony was very special for me. I spoke about my participation in the war and how struggles with that experience brought about my firm convictions about pacifism.

Over the next two years I received invitations to provincial-regional MCC meetings in Manitoba, East Coast (U.S.), Central States (U.S.), Ontario, Alberta, West Coast (U.S.), Great Lakes (U.S.) plus to Mennonite churches in British Columbia and from churches or church groups in the United States. Each spring and fall I was invited to a different region in North America. Altogether I spoke on 180 occasions to approximately 24,000 people.

November 1988: Saskatchewan. After the MCC annual meeting, Erna and I stayed in Saskatchewan. Our travels there for 2,300 kilometres on winter roads were not always enjoyable, but we experienced the Lord's protection. As on all my trips, the audiences were diverse. An example would be when I spoke to an ethics class at the Moose Jaw Roman Catholic High School one morning; the next morning I was at a peace conference at Swift Current Bible Institute, a Mennonite school.

We enjoyed our first assignment in Saskatchewan but Ed Barkman, then Executive Director of MCC Saskatchewan, sensed correctly that it was not always easy. In his evaluation he wrote:

> The response to your presence here has been very positive. Thank you again for sharing your time and energy with us. Thank you also to Erna for spending this time with us as well. I particularly remember Erna's words at our final breakfast together when she talked of the difficulty of having "old wounds reopened" over and over as she listened to you speak. The two weeks spent here were obviously not easy for either of you.

In planning for those preaching-teaching assignments I had prepared seven different topics. On that first trip it became very clear that people wanted to hear my presentation, "Jesus, the Example," based on Hebrews 12:14 which included my own experiences.

March 1989: Manitoba. The experience in Manitoba in March 1989 was very different. Ben Kauenhoven from Bethel Mennonite Church in Winnipeg had offered to drive me to the various meetings. That was a relief because I didn't have to worry about finding the meeting locations.

We had a special evening at the Reinland Community Centre, the oldest Mennonite church building in Manitoba with a pulpit more than 100 years old. Present were representatives from the Blumenorter, Rudnerweider, Evangelical Mennonite Conference (EMC), the Sommerfelder and Old Colony Mennonites. An open and lively question period followed my presentation.

After my address in the Altona Mennonite Church I was approached by a young pastor from one of the neighbouring churches.

I had spoken, as I often did, on forgiveness in connection with my own past. That young pastor knew that one of his church members had been in the Canadian Army and had been involved in street fighting in Italy. His commander had given the order not to take any prisoners, which meant killing every enemy even after they had thrown down their guns and put up their arms. In one house the Canadian soldier encountered a German who had surrendered, but he ran his bayonet into the German soldier's heart. When the German fell, a New Testament covered with blood fell out of his pocket. After 45 years that man was still haunted by the memory of the experience. The young pastor asked me to visit him. He hoped that he could find peace by talking to me, a man who had been on the enemy side during the war.

My schedule did not allow me to go see him but I promised to come back. A few months later I met the young pastor at a conference and told him I would be ready to see his friend at that time. The pastor said that the man had been hospitalized but he would try to get permission from the doctor for me to visit him. The doctor did not allow it because he was concerned that our discussion would do more harm than good. I never did get to see him.

April 1989: U.S. East Coast. Our visit in April 1989 to the MCC East Coast region in the United States was another special experience. For the first time my Ernusch was able to visit Akron, Pennsylvania.

After the second service at the Harrisonburg Mennonite Church in Virginia, Mrs. George Brunk introduced herself to me and spoke warmly about my presentation. We reminisced about the time her husband evangelized in the Fraser Valley area.

At Messiah College near Harrisburg, Pennsylvania, my main emphasis was the lack of biblical basis for the just war theory. After that visit, the campus minister of the school wrote to MCC:

> I felt Siegfried's presentation was excellent. Using story form and scripture he made a powerful case for understanding the development of a pacifist's point of view. . . . The personalized presentation was more powerful in relating to students than other attempts at explaining the Anabaptists' point of view. Siegfried and Erna were delightful guests to have on our campus. I appreciated their willingness to be flexible and to relate on a very open basis.

As we stepped out of the car in the parking lot at Salunga, Pennsylvania, a 15-year-old boy, who had heard my presentation that morning at Lancaster Mennonite High School, stopped for a minute on his way to work. He thanked me for the presentation and said, "Now I know where I stand when I hear all the hammering of the Fundamentalists."

It was especially moving to preach in Blooming Glen, the home church of Clayton Kratz before he went to Russia with the first MCC delegation. He never returned. It was there during the Sunday school hour that my anti-just war theory presentation was most vigorously challenged by a Dutch trainee. That was the only occasion where the war criminal issue came up.

The tour of Lancaster County was very informative. In the 12 years of my membership on the MCC executive committee, I'd never taken the opportunity to be introduced to the Amish community.

At the MCC chapel service in Akron, it was a joyful and moving experience to meet so many friends from my years of MCC involvement. Leaving the Akron area, this time together with Erna, was filled with mixed emotions. During the flight to Sarasota, Florida, we reflected on that experience and our increasing awareness of the wide diversity of Mennonites in Pennsylvania.

That diversity was clearly displayed on Sunday at Sarasota. In the morning service at the Ashton Mennonite Church we experienced the strong charismatic influence. I was grateful that the Holy Spirit

With Erna at Niagara Falls in September 1989 on our trip to Ontario on behalf of MCC.

led me to speak on the *suffering church* worldwide and MCC's part in it, in contrast to the *praising church* we experienced that morning. At the conclusion of the service three people came forward at the altar call and found peace with God.

That evening we were at the Palm Grove Mennonite Church—a church with strong Beachy Amish background. The reverence in that House of God was very evident. In the discussion questions were scriptural and related well to the presentation. We enjoyed a time of personal sharing and fellowship after the service.

September 1989: Ontario. For our assignment in Ontario in September and October 1989 someone had donated a mobile home for us to use during our stay. That arrangement was much nicer for Ernusch who could come and go as she chose.

We spent several days holidaying at Niagara Falls and on Point Pelee, south of Leamington, before we began our service assignment on September 24. What a surprise in Leamington when we unexpectedly ran into our son Gerd who was travelling as fundraiser for the Conference of Mennonites in Canada at the time.

The first of our school visits was at the United Mennonite Educational Institute. For two days I shared my peace message with young people in high schools in the St. Catharines area: Eden Christian College and a private Brethren in Christ school on the Niagara River. Lively discussions always followed my presentations. I was impressed at the thoughtfulness and depth of questions at Eden Christian College when students were given about two minutes to write them down.

At a meeting in the Home for the Aged in Vineland, I reported on the work of MCC around the world. During the discussion time, we talked a lot about the Umsiedler and the situation in Eastern Europe.

Next we moved on to the Kitchener area. We had earlier toured the MCC office there and the SELFHELP warehouse in New Hamburg. The visit to Rockway Mennonite Collegiate was most refreshing. At a roundtable discussion with staff and friends at Conrad Grebel College the next day I addressed what probably was the most highly educated audience to whom I had ever spoken. I enjoyed the dialogue and exchange of ideas.

During that time in Kitchener we had opportunities to visit with a number of people with whom I had been involved in MCC boards. Among them was Helen Epp. It was encouraging to see that she had taken on new responsibilities after Frank's death.

I will never forget the evening with youth of the Aylmer Evangelical Mennonite Mission Conference Church. Their Thanksgiving outing took place at the sand dunes of Lake Erie around a wonderful fire. I shared some life experiences which evoked a lively discussion. The language most commonly understood by the majority in that church was Low German. I do not speak it but was asked to share in the Sunday school hour. They suggested that a mixture of English and High German would be just fine. During the Thanksgiving worship service I combined a message of thankfulness for peace in Canada with my peace testimony.

October 1989: Alberta. During my itineration through some Mennonite churches in Alberta from October 22-30, 1989, I experienced for the first time a Mennonite pastor who was openly opposed to the historic Mennonite peace position. He cited Martin Luther as the basis for his interpretation.

Travelling to the La Crete area in northern Alberta with Bill Thiessen, Director of MCC Alberta, was a special experience. I admired Bill for the way in which he could feel at home with the diverse Mennonite groups there.

March 1990: U.S. West Coast. The trip to MCC West Coast (U.S.) in March 1990 for a shorter period of time included a highlight: a visit to the Mennonite Brethren Seminary in Fresno, California. There the presence of Amnon Shor lent a special flavour to the presentation and discussion. Amnon was a Jew converted to Christianity who was now evangelizing Jews---his curiosity had been aroused by a headline in the local paper announcing my presentation: "Ex-Nazi Preaching on Peace." Amnon had some tough questions and we shared some meaningful thoughts.

One evening I had the privilege of hosting a number of Canadian seminary students and families at a local restaurant. That wonderful gathering was arranged by C.F. Klassen's grandson, Randy.

Both Sundays in California I spoke at churches in the area. The Sunday evening service at the Heritage Bible Church in Bakersfield was the one situation in which I sensed strong opposition to my interpretation of Jesus' stance on peace.

The next Sunday morning service at North Fresno Mennonite Brethren Church was saddened by the announcement of the sudden death the day before of a prominent brother in the membership. He was quite young. I was able to adapt my message on Hebrews 12:14 to the occasion by relating two significant wartime experiences. I

With Amnon Shor in Fresno, California.

followed with the questions: "What would you do if you only had three minutes of life left? Are you prepared to meet the Lord?"

It was interesting to see the very large Mennonite Brethren churches in California. Most of those congregations were very reluctant to deal with the peace teaching issue.

October 1990: U.S. Great Lakes. The MCC Great Lakes (U.S.) region invited me to speak at their annual meeting on October 25-28, 1990. I made three presentations: "Why I Am a Pacifist," "Why Do I Promote MCC?" and "The Joy of Giving." That assignment was special because the chairperson of Great Lakes MCC, Roger Kennell, a farmer in Roanoke, Illinois, had become my friend while we were serving together on MCC boards. We were both farmers with very warm feelings for each other. I stayed at their house and enjoyed their young family.

January 1991: Ohio. In January 1991 the annual meeting of MCC binational was held in Archbold, Ohio. At the public meeting I addressed a youth rally on "Why I Am a Pacifist." Speaking on that theme on the eve of the outbreak of the Gulf War in Iraq was an unforgettable challenge. Communicating with 400 young people in that political climate in the United States could be done only by God's grace.

On the Sunday after that meeting, I was invited to the North Clinton Mennonite Church in Wauseon, Ohio, to speak three times: at the Saturday morning breakfast meeting to mentors of high school kids on the topic, "The Importance of Our Youth Developing Strong Convictions about Peace and Non-resistance to War in Any Form;" at the Sunday morning worship service on "Why I believe in MCC;" and at an afternoon meeting to which area churches had been invited on "My Way to Pacifism." Response from individual listeners was overwhelming. One young man came to me, took my hand in both of his and said: "Thank you for helping me see my way through on the question of pacifism."

In general, I received positive feedback on all my visits sponsored by the provincial and regional MCC bodies—responses like: "You made a deep impression on many listeners. . . . We heard many good comments about your visit to our area. . . . People appreciate your honesty and frankness."

I also made several observations during my travels. Not all agreed with me, but it seemed to me that the biblical position on non-resistance as embraced by Mennonites in the past was in danger of extinction. Part of the reason was that our peace position was seen by many as an obstacle to evangelism. I found that professors and instructors in schools and seminaries had stronger peace and non-resistance positions than many pastors in our churches.

I further noted that our evangelical Mennonite churches were taking verse 19 of Matthew 28 very seriously—making disciples of all nations and baptizing them—but were neglecting verse 20, "teaching them to observe all I have commanded you."

Besides the preaching-teaching assignments on behalf of MCC, several other visits became highlights in our itineration: to the Brethren in Christ conference in summer 1990, to the Elkhart-Goshen area in fall 1991 and to Bethel Church in Winnipeg in fall 1991.

July 1990: Brethren in Christ Conference. At the 1990 Brethren in Christ (BIC) General Conference at Messiah College in Grantham, Pennsylvania, a new statement on militarism was being presented to the delegate body. The emphasis on non-resistance had fairly low priority among the BIC people. I was invited to share something of my testimony at the conference which included most of their pastors plus delegates from congregations—between 500 and 600 people. What a tremendous challenge to address such a gathering. The

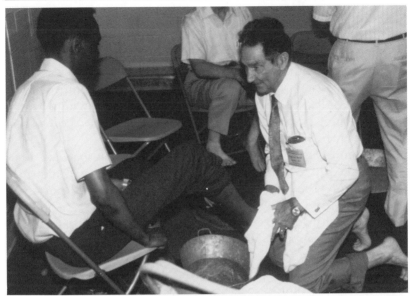

Participation in Footwashing at the Brethren in Christ conference at Messiah College in July 1990.

highlight of my time there was participation in the Footwashing and Lord's Supper. In pairs of two we washed each other's feet. My partner was a brother from Ghana, Africa. In presenting my peace message I used that experience as an example of being brothers even though we did not know each other. What would happen if the governments of our two countries would decide to go to war and asked the two of us to kill each other?

After I returned home Don Shafer, BIC General Secretary, wrote, "You did an outstanding thing for us in boldly and courageously presenting your testimony and reminding us of our biblical call to peace. I felt the Lord used you in a mighty way to address us at a conference where we were facing the very issues that are on your mind and heart."

John K. Stoner, Acting Secretary for MCC's Overseas Peace Office a Brethren in Christ member, wrote, "The challenge to non-violent peacemaking which you gave was a word greatly needed by our conference, and it was given with such passion and clarity that even minds which did not wish to be open to your message were moved."

October 1991: Elkhart-Goshen. On January 15, 1991, Ted Koontz, professor at Associated Mennonite Biblical Seminary (AMBS) in Elkhart, Indiana, invited me to come to AMBS for about one week sometime during the fall semester to be their Theological Center Guest for the 1991-92 school year. We agreed on October 28 to November 1, 1991.

The Sunday before my involvement with the Seminary I was asked to give my peace testimony at the Prairie Street Mennonite Church in Goshen, followed by a 45-minute open discussion with all adult Sunday school classes. Later in the week I spoke at the Goshen College chapel service.

The agenda during the week at Seminary in Elkhart included three chapel talks, three other presentations plus a number of informal dialogues and visits. For my first chapel talk on Monday morning I focused on "My Lifelong Journey to Pacifism." That evening I met with the faculty and gave an informal talk on "The Voice of a Lay Leader in the Church." That was perhaps one of the most difficult topics, but later two of the professors encouraged me to review some of my points with the students, which I did in my last presentation at the Friday morning chapel.

Another demanding assignment was speaking at a Forum on Thursday to the largest audience during my time at the Seminary. Ted Koontz asked me to speak about "the experience of the churches in Germany in giving up pacifism and being sucked into nationalism" and how that relates to what I saw in North America. I developed the pilgrimage of the Mennonites in North Germany from 1914 to 1918, the official change of the North German Mennonite Conference in 1932 and subsequent developments during the Second World War. An intense discussion followed. In my closing statement I made the point that Mennonites churches in North America were in danger of going the same way in embracing American patriotism as evidenced by the American flag in many churches.

For the final chapel my topic was "Reflections for Future Pastors of an Unordained Lay Leader in the Mennonite Church." I began with a quote by George Bernard Shaw, "Every profession is a conspiracy against the laity," followed by a strong condemnation of Mennonite pastors who used the title Reverend. I quoted from an article by Harry Wilson in *Presbyterian Life* (1962), "Let's Call Ministers Ministers." He maintains that "to break down the *reverend* idea and to remove the separation between preacher and the people," the whole church, not just the clergyman, must be holy, separated unto God; "the whole church lives by faith and grace." I used Psalm 111:9, "Holy and reverend is his name" to show that God alone is reverend, that it is clearly unbiblical to use the term Reverend for an ordained minister. In closing, I quoted from R. Paul Stevens' book, *Liberating the Laity*: "Our seminaries . . . are not only failing to prepare the clergy for their role of equipping, but they are also supporting a philosophy which depreciates a theology of the laity. . . . Thus, the theologians inadvertently define what the church institution really is" (Stevens, 86).

November 1991: Bethel Mennonite Church. In summer 1991, Gerald Gerbrandt from Bethel Mennonite Church in Winnipeg invited me to speak at their fund-raising banquet that November. They had built a new sanctuary and still needed considerable money to pay for the building. I told Gerald that I was the wrong man to speak about raising funds for a church building, but I would gladly speak on one of my favourite topics, "The Joy of Giving." We agreed on November 16 as the date for my visit. It was a joy to relate my convictions about giving for the Lord. The fact that our son Dietrich and wife Jocelyn were in the congregation added a personal note to my testimony. The thank you letter which I received from the chairperson of Bethel Church after that weekend ended with, "We wish you God's continued rich blessings as you write your book."

67. Reflections of an Unordained Person

My October 1991 experience at the Seminary brought to the fore all the struggles I had over the years regarding ordained people and the organized church. I remember with some bitterness when, as a boy, I saw Vati, my father, standing *beside* the pulpit when he was preaching at youth rallies in my home church. For me Vati was the symbol of a truly Christian man. He was an excellent preacher but was never elected to the lay ministry—the church at that time had lay ministers only. Because of the way in which my father was treated, I had to struggle with the organized church which had said, "Your father is not the man for us." In my mind that comment was an unforgivable sin. That message, which I received when I was a teenager, haunted me throughout my life.

When I was 15 or 16 years old I had reservations about the procedures leading up to baptism. During catechism instruction for four to six months, the qualifying test for baptism was memorizing the answers to printed questions in the catechism. I often wondered about Acts 2:41 "So those who received his word were baptized, and there were added that day about three thousand souls." I was baptized and did join the organized church. Perhaps it was inevitable that even today I am considered to be somewhat of an outsider in the church.

It was *not* strange that, over a long period of my life, in the eyes of the *world* I had been seen as an outsider. I was considered as someone who was extremely spiritual. All my comrades in the German Army knew that the Bible was my steady companion and that I prayed regularly. Also, when the chaplain of the Division could not be present, I as an officer was asked to say the table grace at official gatherings.

Now my struggles were with being an outsider in the *church* and with the temptation of ordained persons to exercise undue power within that church. We experienced one example when, after arriving in Canada, we attended the Mennonite Brethren Church in Yarrow with our hosts, the David Rempels. The leadership, all lay ministers, ruled that church with an iron hand. Ernusch and I could not understand nor accept that we were not allowed to take part in the Lord's Supper.

When we had our own church group shortly after we arrived in Agassiz, no one was ordained. We were all equals. That changed when we joined the East Chilliwack Mennonite Church. When the pastor of the congregation visited our home before we were interviewed for membership, the questioning was intense and unpleasant. I remember very clearly his comment that he could not see himself taking part in any action where the intent was to kill someone. At that time I was not yet at the place where I am now in my spiritual pilgrimage. I responded, "You must realize that in making the decision to be active in the army, you must also be prepared to *be* killed."

For a short time after that interview I was ready to forget about church----the organized church. I was turned off by the spiritual arrogance of the ordained person, the reign of the "holy ones." Yet I knew I could not do that to my father who, together with my mother, was joining the church at the same time. I knew I could not withhold the church experience, mainly Sunday school, from our sons. So we joined, in spite of the fact that Ernusch and I were extremely hurt in the process of becoming members.

The congregation must have been desperate for leadership. Even though I was a newcomer, I was elected to be congregational and church council chairperson. With the help of an excellent secretary, we managed to conduct the meetings in a businesslike manner. Certainly the input of the pastor, the ministers and deacons were important in spiritual concerns, but they were not given a special say in matters like the construction of the new church building. I met some opposition when I insisted that the term, Pastor, replace Reverend in the minutes of council meetings.

During my pilgrimage in church life I encountered four kinds of spiritual arrogance: the arrogance of being ordained, the arrogance of organizational power, the arrogance of intellect and the arrogance of being educated (but not necessarily wise). All have one element in common: disobedience to Christ's teaching, "It shall not be so among you; but whoever would be great among you must be your servant" (Matthew 20:26).

Sometimes I wondered if my interpretation of the attitude of the ordained toward the unordained was exaggerated. But one day my view was confirmed. I was talking with an ordained deacon about one brother who had gone into voluntary service for a term. The deacon said, "The church where this brother is a member should have ordained him for his time in service. Now when he comes back he will be a 'nobody.'"

That deacon brother did not realize that, in one sense, I also was "a nobody." But, by the grace of God, I had been able to serve, despite the fact that I was never ordained. My first opportunities to speak in the British Columbia churches came when I became a board member of the Mennonite Benevolent Society. After that, the involvements increased. In my posts on the MCC boards, I became acceptable to the ordained as a speaker on MCC and related issues.

The change at Eden came when one of the lay ministers died and a shortage of preachers who could speak in the German language became acute. I was asked to be part of the German preaching team in 1972, but when I was invited a year later to be a deacon candidate, I refused. By that time "my plate was full" with MCC work.

I knew that the Lord had called me to serve in the areas where I was involved. I was reminded of the words of Joseph to his brothers: "It was not you who sent me here, but God" (Genesis 45:8). The Lord had given me many responsibilities in his kingdom even though I was outside the circle of "the ordained."

I experienced the break-down of the ordained-unordained categories during my years on the executive committee of MCC. Those are my most wonderful memories of work within organized church structures. There relationships with college presidents, university and college professors, ministers of the gospel or lay people like me were ideal. We were equals, a wonderful example and model of Christian community.

My struggle with the place of an unordained person in the church was always bound up with my questions about the state of our Mennonite churches. We claim to be part of the Believers' Church tradition which, according to the 1974 statement on ordination of the General Conference Mennonite Church, means "that all members are priests or ministers to each other and to those not yet in the church . . . that all members are ministers of God and called to discipleship through baptism . . . and that there are occasions when any Christian can minister mercy and grace to another person."

I believe that's a myth. The Mennonite churches, just like most evangelical churches, have moved away from that principle. In the New Testament passages quoted in the above document, none give advice on or sanction the profession of ordained ministry. R. Paul Stevens in *Liberating the Laity* writes:

> Vancouver scholar Marjorie Warkentin concluded that the vocabulary of New Testament leadership permits no pyramidal forms; it is the language of horizontal relationships. . . . Ordination can have no function in such a system, for it sets up barriers, where none should exist; that is, between one Christian and another, and hinders the mutual service by which the church is edified (15).

I acknowledge that I met many wonderful servants of Christ in the church among the group of the ordained. However, a large pool of willing lay workers remains dormant within the majority of our congregations. It is my prayer that our churches will find ways to give more room to the power of the Holy Spirit and the gifts within its laity.

What I considered the best example of service by the unordained was the women who survived the rule of Communism in Russia. Millions of Christian men had been taken away from their families, most of them never to return. The women carried the torch of Christianity through that time of hardship. When the Umsiedler from Russia started arriving in Germany, only very few older men came with them. The leadership role in the churches of their new homeland was taken over by the younger generation of men from the hands of their unordained, praying mothers.

Here in North America I have noticed that the more the local church turns inward, the less interest it shows in proclaiming the Lord's kingdom to the world. In our home church and other churches it seems that participation in Bible studies, not behaviour and actions

An unordained person preaching from the pulpit. "By the grace of God, I had been able to serve, despite the fact that I was never ordained."

outside the church, is the main measurement for evaluating spirituality. A new Bible study group is praised and publicized with a great deal of fanfare, but no mention is made, for example, of young church women who are active in homes for battered women, working in "the name of Christ." When our youngest son, Martin, and his friends started a drop-in centre to minister to street kids, his (our) home church did not even recognize it. There was no prayer or financial support for them. When, as chairperson of the public school board, I was involved with the Doukhobors and tried to bring peace to the turbulent situation, only a few church members were concerned about my work.

If the church of Jesus Christ will not learn anew what Jesus meant when he said, "You are the salt of the *earth*" (Matthew 5:13), not "You are the salt of the *church*," the church will lose its credibility. It will have no message to the world. For the world to believe, it must see Christianity in action.

68. The Road to Forgiveness

Time and time again I was encouraged to write down my experiences. Now I have done so, but the story is not finished. I've written about what happened to me when I was growing up and while I was at war; about my wonderful family and my experiences in farming;

about my struggles with the organized church and my opportunities for service in the wider church setting; about how other people enriched my life during my travels in North America and beyond. The story yet to be told is how God led me on the path to freedom.

My life began with mother asking God's blessing on it. For me and my siblings, Reichfelde, our childhood home in Prussia, became a heaven on earth. Our parents were models of love and compassion and we joyfully accepted their spiritual values as our own. Evangelistic meetings at our house and, as we grew older, involvement in active church life reinforced what we had been taught in our home.

Our parents never pushed us to declare our acceptance of the Lord as our personal Saviour. For most of us, as in my case, that conviction became self-evident. The day of baptism was the occasion to make a public statement. It did not seem necessary for me to know the occasion and the exact hour when I was "born again."

I had committed my life to Christ at baptism, but I wept about my behaviour many times in my life. I chose to mark one occasion when my father reprimanded me for my treatment of a farm worker as my new beginning. Even though I needed to make other new beginnings after that, it was that moment when I confirmed my decision to follow Christ.

The assurance that I was a child of God remained a deep conviction throughout my pilgrimage—yes, even when I joined the army. During my time in the army I never experienced oppression or scorn for being a Christian, for reading the Bible or for spending time in prayer. In fact the opposite was true. Throughout all my years in the army, fellow soldiers came to talk to me, seeking help with their personal struggles.

Two incidents early on during the war started me on a journey which changed my life. One was my first confrontation with a wounded, German-speaking soldier from the enemy camp who could have been my cousin. The other was when I listened in on Russian soldiers, the enemy, as they sang Christmas carols in the trenches.

Those experiences affected me deeply, but at that time did not influence my conviction in regard to serving in the army. Any doubts I might have had were wiped away by feelings of patriotism and by an interpretation of Romans 13 based on Martin Luther's. The position of our Mennonite forefathers did not seem relevant for the present. I excused them with, "They did not know better."

That attitude provided me with strength during the war and in struggles immediately after the war. I was more philosophical about the senselessness of war in general than about my personal involve-ment in it.

I could not see then, as I do now, that serving in the army was really participation in professional killing. The treatment of German civilians by the victorious allies, mainly Russians, and the stories about the millions of women who were raped by the Russians, were not convincing enough for me to pursue a position of non-resistance.

After the war, we began receiving *Der Bote*, the German-language newspaper of the General Conference Mennonites, in our home. At first we were shocked about some of the writings. German Menno-nites, especially those from West Prussia, were condemned, actually scolded in a satirical manner. The only ray of light in regard to contact with the world of the victorious allies was the involvement of Mennonite Central Committee. C.F. Klassen came to Germany to look for "the lost Mennos." Brother C.F. was from a nation which was considered our enemy. The war had just ended and, in a very direct way, he showed us Matthew 5:44 in action: "Love your enemies and pray for those who persecute you."

C.F. was also the man who gave my brother Hans and me special advice when we boarded the *Beaverbrae* for the voyage to Canada. He cautioned us not to speak up too quickly about matters related to farming in the new country. "Be silent for five years," he said. "Thereafter speak up." That was in 1951.

By 1957 I began to speak in a very different setting when I accepted the congregational chairmanship of the East Chilliwack Mennonite Church. In the 1960s I started teaching Sunday school and began preaching in 1972. Yet it was in my service beyond the walls of the local church that I experienced my second conversion, my conversion to pacifism.

Until one day during the war, I had found it fairly easy to justify participation in war on the basis of Romans 13, "be subject to the governing authorities." But as time went on, I could not defend my own action in that dark hour in Russia when I had given the order to have one young man executed. Even though my action was endorsed by the security personnel, the order had come from me, from me alone.

What then was the difference between that action and the normal battle activities of an ordinary soldier? For me, there was an incredible difference. That was not killing in combat. *I* had ordered his execu-tion. Clearly *I* was guilty of killing that man. When I entered that "guilty plea," I came to a new understanding of Romans 13 and found my way to the cross with a renewed sense of joy.

It was when I became a member of MCC Canada and we began the dialogue on capital punishment in 1972 that I felt compelled to assess my own past actions and gave a public testimony of my struggles. The MCC circle of friends was willing to listen to my story, to try and understand. They helped me in my search for the biblical answer to my struggles. I came to Hebrews 12:14, "Strive for peace with all and the holiness without which no one will see the Lord." I heard in a new way Jesus' words, "For I have given you an example, that you also should do as I have done to you" (John 13:15).

In accepting those truths, it became crystal clear to me that Jesus' teaching in the Sermon on the Mount needed to be taken literally: "But I say to you, Love your enemies and pray for those who persecute you. . . . Therefore you must be perfect, as your heavenly Father is perfect" (Matthew 5: 44, 48). That left no room for participation in war. You cannot love your enemy *and* pull the trigger.

My thinking had changed gradually, but I failed to share my growing insights with my loved ones, especially with Ernusch. When I started to speak out on the topic, my wonderful life companion always found excuses for my past actions. She loved me so much that she did not want to see me "pleading guilty."

I heard her argue many times, "You soldiers protected us, especially us women, from inhumane treatment by Russian soldiers. We were so thankful for the protection we received when we fled from our homeland to the West. We all knew what happened to the ones who fell into their hands."

Although I could not refute that argument, my answer was a personal one, "Yes, but you had no part in our attack on Poland or the U.S.S.R. You were not there on that black day when I ordered my subordinate to execute that young man. Just like I can hardly imagine what you experienced when you gave birth to our seven sons, you can share only a small fraction of my experience."

It was at the annual meeting of MCC Saskatchewan on November 11, 1988, that I first spoke publicly about my change in convictions. None in the audience could imagine what a shock it was for my Ernusch to hear me dealing publicly with my guilt.

After pleading guilty before God, I had received unlimited freedom to teach and to preach. My nightmares—seeing that young man standing before God, pointing his finger at me—were gone. I had found forgiveness for all my wrongdoing. The guilt was gone but I

would have to continue living with some of the pain for the rest of my life. Ross W. Marrs has said, "Take away my capacity for pain and you rob me of the possibility for joy."

I always knew that God would forgive unconditionally. But I never, never would have expected that admitting guilt, speaking publicly about failure, sin and forgiveness would lead to such wonderful freedom—freedom to move forward with God and to continue serving God's people.

Looking Ahead

For over 40 years my beloved Ernusch and I have lived in the mountains near Agassiz. Here we raised our six sons and made a living by farming. The Lord has accompanied me on my life's journey of 80 years, sometimes over rocky roads.

The path took me over ever-changing terrain: from being born in West Prussia to thriving in Canada, from being a soldier to becoming a pacifist, from surviving as a refugee to achieving success as a farmer, from wandering as an immigrant to entering local politics, from involvement in a B.C. Mennonite church to helping shape policies in an inter-Mennonite, binational organization, from enjoying family life to being thrust into third world affairs—and from struggling with the pain of guilt to accepting the freedom of forgiveness.

In 1994 at our mountain home in Aggasiz.

I look back and remember with thanksgiving the joy and the pain, the disappointments and the opportunities, the struggle and the victory. But I also move forward with faith and hope.

Once again I look out over the mountains and see life pass before my eyes. I have recalled the past, but as I contemplate the future these mountains remind me of God's steadfastness. They may obstruct my view but, despite rocky obstacles, if I follow the path I will reach the other side of the mountain. And God will be with me, no matter where that journey takes me in the future.

Words of Thanksgiving

In my chapters on Mennonite Central Committee and church life I may have overemphasized difficult situations. That was done to show the reader something about the wide-ranging responsibilities with which board members had to deal. Despite some difficult times, I have enjoyed all my involvements.

Some readers, family members and others will find occasions which they remember differently than I did. Some situations may not be reported accurately. My capacity for doing research work was limited and my ability to recollect has human limitations. I ask for your indulgence.

There will be stories that I should have included as belonging to my pilgrimage—of some I am already aware—therefore I ask for your pardon in my judgement of choices.

Altogether, my heart is overflowing with thankfulness for a variety of reasons. First, I am thankful to the Lord that he reached down to me, that I became his child, that he protected me through all the war years and also in peace time, in spite of many close calls during my life. I am thankful for good health.

I am thankful to God for my parents, for the model they have been, for their prayers and guidance. I am thankful to the Lord for my brothers and sisters who were instrumental in helping me remember Reichfelde as a heaven on earth.

I am deeply thankful that God gave me such a wonderful marriage partner, my Ernusch. During wartime I was able to pour out my heart to her in thousands of letters. She became the mother of our seven sons (six still living). She made our home an oasis of warmth and care during turbulent times. She taught the boys their first prayer and continued to be a spiritual fountain for them. She showed deep understanding for their struggles, even at those times when I tried to be more firm.

Ernusch was a strong supporter of my involvements in public and church life. When I was away from the farm and family for many, many evenings, sometimes for several weeks at a time, it was reassur-